BULLDOG

BULLDOG

The world's most famous truck

by John B. Montville

A Transportation Series Book By:
AZTEX Corporation—Tucson, AZ 85703

Cover art by Robert E. Schulz

Book design by John M. Peckham

ISBN 0-89404-008-1

Library of Congress Catalog Card No: 78-56336

Printed in the United States of America

AZTEX Corporation
Tucson, Arizona 85703

Foreword

by
Henry Austin Clark, Jr.

When I was a boy growing up in Flushing, Long Island, we had a sort of game trying to identify the trucks as they came along our road. The trick was to call out the make before the truck was in sight, using the sound of the truck as a clue. The shaft drive trucks sounded different from those with chain drive, and the various engines also had their individual sounds. The very flat exhaust of the Pierce-Arrow was easy to spot, the double reduction gears of the big Whites had sort of a rattle, but the one that nobody could mistake was the Bulldog Mack, with its gutteral exhaust bark and singing of the drive chains.

Of course there were dozens of different makes of trucks, light and heavy, and many of them could not be named without a closer inspection where the name could be read. In those days, the 1920s, there was a great deal of construction going on in Flushing, and the huge excavations for the basements of apartment houses posed a severe problem for the dump trucks of the day. Of all the trucks that were used on these jobs, one was head and shoulders over the others in performance. That truck was the Model AC Mack, with it radiator mounted behind the engine, rather than in front like almost all the others. One day, I resolved, I would be able to drive one of these great monsters.

Eventually that day did come, when I purchased a 1924 flat bed truck that had worked the docks in Manhattan, and was for sale for a reasonable price on a used truck lot in Long Island City. How did I get it home to Southampton, where it was to live? Drive it, of course! It took quite a while, but it ran like a top, and the journey was lots of fun. There is no feeling of power like driving a Bulldog Mack truck.

Over twenty-five years ago, a young man whom I had met in the old car hobby took a summer job at the Long Island Automotive Museum in Southampton. From the first day on the job it was evident that his main interest lay with antique trucks, rather than old cars. He seemed happiest working on the restoration of a 1921 Autocar two-cylinder chassis, a project under way in the Museum shop.

The previous year he had been working in the advertising department of the Mack company in New York City. During this period they were closing up the Long Island City Plant. John Montville discovered that the entire file of 8 x 10 inch glass plate and film photographic negatives was about to be thrown out. These negatives covered every model of every Mack and Saurer truck from 1914 on. (The International Motor Company had built the Swiss-designed Saurer truck in New Jersey in those days.) John was able to persuade his boss that these invaluable files should be preserved, and so they were given to our Museum. We loaded a truck and a station wagon with seventy-six transfer cases which were placed in the Museum archives, and not destroyed like those of Packard, a few years later.

In the years that followed John became even more interested in Mack history. He spent many hours in the archives, arranging and studying the negatives, and having photographic prints made up. It was not long before he had decided to write a book on Mack, and that is just what he did. The project took uncounted hours of work, even before the writing process, but the result was *Mack*, the most definitive history of any make of truck.

Now, a few years later, years when John has spent many more hours in the stacks, another book has emerged. This one, *Bulldog: The World's Most Famous Truck*, is more closely focused on the Truck that built America between the two World Wars, the Bulldog Mack.

Henry Austin Clark, Jr.

Dedication

To Alfred Fellows Masury, 1882 - 1933, the one person truly
deserving of the title, "Mr. Bulldog."

Contents

Preface

For those readers wishing to know the necessity for another book on the subject of Mack trucks, I feel that a few words of explanation are in order.

When my first work on the corporate and product history of Mack Trucks, Inc. was completed, it was quite obvious to those involved with the project that much information dealing with the famous Bulldog truck had to be left out due to space limitations in *Mack*. Both my publisher, Walter R. Haessner, and the designer-illustrator, John M. Peckham, shared the feeling that basic public interest in the Bulldog Mack warranted another book. It was therefore agreed that a second work should be researched, using additional data and photos to tell the story of the development of the most outstanding of all heavy-duty trucks.

Further research uncovered the fascinating life of the Bulldog's master designer and major promoter, Alfred Fellows Masury, Mack's chief engineer between 1914 and 1933. A. F. Masury's colorful career in the motor truck industry was characterized by his unlimited energy and the influence of his ideas on the people and products with which he came in contact. An understanding of the background, character, and ideals of A. F. Masury will also help to explain the development of the Bulldog truck.

In unfolding the Bulldog story, it was quite vital to indicate the state of the trucking industry at various stages, and the Bulldog's place in each. Changes in the Bulldog's mechanical design have been detailed, hopefully not to the boredom of the more casual reader. The rationale behind most of the changes made during its almost quarter century of manufacture have been indicated whenever possible. It was also considered necessary to deal somewhat with the progress of the Mack organization during the Bulldog era, while trying to avoid repeating information contained in the first book, *Mack*.

Information dealing with certain aspects of the Bulldog's production, construction, and preservation, has been detailed in six separate sections of the Appendix. A brief history of the Mack corporate symbol and mascot, which were inspired by the popularity of the Bulldog truck, is followed by a run-down on some of the trucks still in use and being preserved in various collections. A table of comparative specifications of the different Bulldog versions, and dimensional diagrams of these, as well as a listing of chassis numbers, are presented for those wishing this type of technical data for restoration and model making purposes. Finally, a listing of all known Bulldog toy trucks and miniatures has been developed for those interested in collecting the scaled-down version of the actual truck.

No work of this magnitude and complexity is possible without the help of many people and organizations. My publisher, Aztex Corporation, has been kept in a state of suspense concerning this work while the author moved, and took care of sundry other projects, including the gathering of many additional photos for the book. However, their backing of this project was the first and most important step in a long chain of events leading to the successful conclusion of this project.

As with my first work, E. A. Hanauer, former Mack engineer, provided the vital technical expertise, proofreading, and gadfly services necessary to keeping the project on the right track. Without El's advice and counsel the Bulldog story would have been less accurate and more superficial, at best.

Other individuals who provided important information on certain aspects of early Mack history are: Jack Winchester, former fleet supervisor and early associate of A. F. Masury; John A. Sloan, former Mack branch manager and associate of A. F. Masury; Henry Miller, Mack executive engineer, retired; A. C. Fetzer, veteran Mack sales executive; and Perry Hooker, Bulldog Mack fancier extraordinaire.

Specific information on early Cummins diesels was provided by John W. Rowell of the Cummins Engine Company. Data and graphic material on the development of bodies for off-highway trucks was supplied by Arnold F. Meyer and Paul Miller, respectively, of the Heil Company. Information on the use of aluminum in the Boulder Dam truck bodies was supplied by J. M. Arnold and W. C. Weltman of the Aluminum Company of America. An analysis of Sterling chain-drive trucks as competitors to the Bulldog in the late 1920s, was supplied by E. R. Sternberg, former chief engineer of Sterling Motor Truck Co., Inc. William D. Brown provided both information on and photos of the huge Bulldog sign built by the Federal Sign Division for Mack's world head-quarters building. And James Daniels provided construction details and graphics relating to the Rockefeller Center project of the early 1930s.

Special mention must be made of the efforts made by Mike Pietraroia in producing the fine dimensional diagrams reproduced in the Appendix. Also, John T. West spent much time in researching the extensive listing of toys, as well as the introduction thereto, found in the last section of the Appendix. The author spent a seemingly endless amount of time in various parts of the Research Division of the New York Public Library, and without the access to these facilities this book would have been impossible to complete properly.

I am also indebted to the following people for the graphics they provided: Bill Hall, Orlando, Fla.; H. Keith Smith, Anna Maria, Fla.;C. P. Fox, Winter Haven, Fla.; Bob Magnotta, Hartsdale, N. Y.; Henry Austin Clark, Jr., Glen Cove, N. Y.; Bill West, Westlake Village, Calif.; James B. Bibb, Dearborn Heights, Mich.; Virgil White, Los Angeles, Calif.; George Humphrey, Gray, Maine; Steve Heaver, Jr., Baltimore, Md.; Daniels & Kennedy, New York, N. Y.; and John W. Geipe, Baltimore, Md. Special credit is also due the staff of Rotocopy, Inc., New York, which provided many of the quality photographic prints used in this work.

To all those not mentioned, but who provided a small service or encouraging word to help the project along, a grateful "Thank You."

John B. Montville
May 3, 1979

THE "BULLDOG" Mack
1 — 1½ — 2
3½ — 5½ — 7½
TONS CAPACITY
Write to Dept. 2
for Catalog
INTERNATIONAL
MOTOR COMPANY
New York

PERFORMANCE COUNTS

9

BULLDOG

1912-1919 |1
Background and birth—
The Bulldog and his pedigree|

Inspirations

The basic roots of the Bulldog Mack truck go back several years before its actual road testing in 1915. Having a knowledge of the people responsible and the circumstances surrounding its conception will make the unparalleled success of this famous vehicle more understandable. An incident remembered many years later by one of the participants is the best starting point for this fascinating story of men and machines.[1]

"Look at the way that new bus pulls away from the curb and keeps right up with traffic, Jack," observed the Sunday after noon stroller to his companion. The two men agreed that a ride was then necessary in order to observe the vehicle's characteristics more closely, so they quickly boarded at the corner stop. As the bus headed determinedly up New York's Fifth Avenue, the pair casually watched the throng in its latest 1912 finery, but eagerly observed the driver's use of the gears and the vehicle's response to his manipulations. So impressed were the two men, that a round trip was taken, and the younger man, Jack, offered to make a visit to the garage for a closer inspection and report.

What had so impressed the two was an imported French vehicle, a De Dion - Bouton, a make which the Fifth Avenue Coach Company had finally used in 1907 to replace its old horse-drawn stages after other motor vehicles had proved unequal to the task. The new De Dion chassis had been introduced to the streets of Paris only a few months before the New York bus line

The famous bulldog, always a willing worker, is shown here with a payload of 14 tons of wool. This 1919 photo, taken in the Boston, Mass. area, shows how much in the way of weight and bulk that the Mack AC owners were tempted to pile on their stalwart helper.

had ordered one for a trial period.[2] One unusual characteristic of the 1912 chassis was the round radiator design. With the new design, called the Solex type, the fan had an unobstructed access to ambient air which it could force through the two surrounding radiator sections.

The leader of the two men was Alfred F. Masury, a mechanical engineer with an intimate knowledge of heavy vehicle construction, having helped design the first gasoline propelled 10-ton trucks built in the United States several years before. His younger associate, John F. "Jack" Winchester, also had many credits in the field of heavy truck construction and operation, and was then a mechanical inspector for the International Motor Company where the two men worked. Masury's keen interest in the new bus prompted Winchester to offer his time in taking measurements of one of its features. And upon arrival at the bus garage Jack was directed to the bus company's chief engineer, George Green.

The imported 1912 French motor bus which starred in a fateful Sunday afternoon ride on New York's Fifth Avenue. Note unusual circular shape of radiator on the De Dion Bouton single deck bus.

Although only recently arrived in America, George Green had a thorough grounding in motor vehicle design through his association with pioneer bus operations in Great Britain.[3] The two men had no problem getting to the point of the young man's visit, since they both belonged to the Society of Automobile Engineers, (later Society of Automotive Engineers) and were soon engrossed in a discussion of the De Dion's specifications. However, Green balked when Winchester asked permission to disassemble the radiator to measure the size of its tubes in relation to its water capacity and engine size, claiming that he could. not spare the bus from the route. However, when Winchester stated he would come back and stay all night if need be, Green, being so impressed with Jack's nerve and determination, assigned a mechanic to help speed the task!

What had started out as just a Sunday stroll turned into an engineering field trip, and an example of one man's determination to get the details about all those things which aroused his curiosity. This man, Alfred Fellows Masury, known to his friends as "Red," or "Red Mike," due to the flaming red hair of his youth, would earn the respect and loyalty of his close associates in the next score of years. However, at this point in his career Masury had many challenges to his talent, training, and tenacity, and how he met them will give a good insight on how the truck industry survived and grew in its formative years.

Overcoming A Crisis

Masury's employer at the start of 1912 was the Hewitt Motor Company of New York City, but through a merger during March of that year he found himself with the recently organized International Motor Company. The latter firm was the result of the merger, in the fall of 1911, of the pioneer Mack Brothers Motor Car Company of Allentown, Pennsylvania, and the Swiss-licensed Saurer Motor Company of Plainfield, New Jersey. Since the early 1900s the commercial vehicles built by the Mack Brothers had achieved a fine reputation for strength and durability, but rising demand necessitated additional plant facilities, and consequently the merger was arranged by a large Wall Street Banking house that apparently had a financial stake in the Saurer operation. The Saurer Motor Company had received strong backing from prominent financial interests in its bid to produce, on a license agreement, a heavy-duty truck of quality design originated by the firm of Adolph Saurer A.G., Arbon, Switzerland.[4]

The Hewitt Motor Company, formed in 1905 by Edward R. Hewitt, grandson of the famous American inventor and philanthropist, Peter Cooper, had earned a reputation for producing highly engineered trucks. The original factory was a converted three story livery stable on East 31st Street, but as the size of the truck increased some of the work had to be jobbed out. In 1908 and 1909 the new 10-ton models were built under contract in Peabody, Massachusetts, at the plant of the Machine Sales Company, and during the 1910 to 1911 period by P. H. Gill & Sons of Brooklyn, New York.[5]

A native of New England, J. F. Winchester was employed in the construction of the first Hewitt 10-ton trucks, and then transferred to the Hewitt Motor Company in New York when the first contract ran out. After the merger Winchester continued in various assignments, including inspection and service work on Mack, Saurer, and Hewitt trucks operating in the New York metropolitan area. This work during 1912 brought him into contact with the early fleet operators, such as breweries, coal merchants, and petroleum companies. Early in 1913 he accepted a job offer from the Standard Oil Company of New Jersey, and was soon placed in charge of their growing fleet of trucks.

What followed in the wake of the Hewitt merger in 1912 can best be described as a struggle between the various financial interests which had backed the separate companies. Also, the founders of the Mack and Hewitt companies, along with their engineering staffs, had their own concepts of design which they naturally wished to see continued in the trucks built by the new concern. However, the first president of the International Motor Company was C. P. Coleman, a mechanical engineer who was president of the Saurer Motor Company, and it was his ideas that predominated at first. Coleman had been in charge of the Singer Building construction in 1905, one of New York's early skyscrapers.[6] Charles W. Stratford, who had been associated with Coleman on a project in 1911 to exploit a rotary valve automobile engine of French origin, was made chief engineer of the International Motor Company.

Stratford's specialty was engine design and lubrication engineering, and his first important project for the new company was the development of a new line of trucks having a monobloc type engine design. The monobloc was a radical departure from the cast-in-pair cylinder block engines produced previously by Mack, Saurer, and Hewitt. And serious problems would beset the new company before Stratford's project could be concluded.

The year 1913 became a crucial one for the Intenational Motor Company, as a business recession caught the new com-

Alfred Fellows Masury stands between two officials of the Machine Sales Company, builders under contract of this five-ton Hewitt truck in 1908.

pany with much of its capital committed to an expansionist policy. Compounding the effects of the recession had been the entrance of several quality automobile producers into the heavy-duty truck market through their well established dealer networks. Pierce-Arrow, Peerless, and Locomobile had introduced heavy truck lines during 1911 and 1912, adding fierce competition to Packard's already successful three-ton model introduced late in 1908. Added to this was White's large gasoline propelled trucks joining its steam and gas automobile line at the end of 1909.

The pressure on the automobile dealers to dispose of their truck allocations resulted in many extravagant deals, which had the net effect of cutting profit margins throughout the commercial vehicle industry. The repercussions were profound, with one trade publication reporting that 36 new makes would be on the truck market in 1914 to only partly replace the 44 makes which were discontinued in 1913.[7]

An effort to conserve the International's capital caused the firm to miss its last 1912 quarterly dividend on preferred stock,[8] and then seek additional financing from various sources during

The Hewitt 10-ton truck, designed in 1909, became popular in the coal and brewery trades in New York City by 1912.

1913. It was not until some of the influential backers of the Hewitt Motor Company asserted themselves that a sound restructuring of the company began to take place. Ambrose Monell, who had been the main backer of E. R. Hewitt when the new Hewitt Motor Company was being constituted late in 1911, became chairman of the board of directors in the spring of 1913.[9] The original president of the International Motor Company, C. P. Coleman, resigned in June, and a general reorganization of both administration and product gradually followed. Coleman's successor was John Calder, another manager with an engineering background, but he only lasted three months, being replaced by Vernon Monroe, the company's former secretary.[10] During this period only one new truck model embracing the Stratford monobloc engine design was introduced before work was suspended on the rest of the new truck models, due to their high production cost.

The Hewitt Legacy

A keystone in the revamped organization was the huge service station and headquarters building at West End Avenue, between 63rd and 64th Streets, just west of what is today New York City's famous Lincoln Center area. The original section of this structure had been acquired by the Hewitt organization early in 1912, just prior to the merger, but at a total investment of nearly $1 million a big enlargement project was completed during the summer of 1913.[11] While the prime function of the six-story building was the servicing of Mack, Saurer, and Hewitt trucks, adequate room was allocated on the top floors for general offices, and the engineering and experimental departments. And it seemed only logical that A. F. Masury, the former factory manager of the Hewitt Motor Company, be placed in charge of the huge service operation.

Masury's first move was to make the service function a separate operation, designed to be self-supporting, and no longer an auxiliary of the sales department. In this way top management could also monitor the actual use of the company's product, seeing that customers got proper service and that warranties were not abused. Separate teams of mechanics were assigned to each of the three makes of trucks produced by the company.[12] Trucks were completely torn down and rebuilt, when deemed necessary, all under the watchful eyes of practical but innovative engineers and master mechanics. The whole operation was soon systematized and running smoothly, due in no small part to Masury's determination to put the company's service function on both a production and paying basis. The successful reorganization of the service department by the end of 1913 was only the first of many contributions that A. F. Masury would make to the Mack organization in the years to come.

With the resignation of C. W. Stratford late in 1913, Edward Ringwood Hewitt became chief engineer. E. R. Hewitt was a graduate chemical engineer who combined a natural talent for mechanics with a knowledge of metallurgy, with the resulting products of his company being of unique design and high quality. A son of Abram S. Hewitt, mayor of New York in the late 1880's, E. R. Hewitt's maternal grandfather was Peter Cooper, who is credited with building America's first steam locomotive, and later with founding Cooper Union, the famous school in New York City for engineering, art, and design.[13]

A number of talented engineers and mechanics had become associated with the old Hewitt Motor Company, with the original Hewitt engineering and production staff including among others the following people: Alfred F. Masury, Maximilian C. Frins, August H. Leipert, and John F. Winchester. August H. "Gus" Leipert had apparently been associated with the Hewitt family enterprises even before the formation of the Hewitt Motor Company in 1905. Gus Leipert was Hewitt's original machine shop superintendent, being a meticulous worker who contributed many improvements to the products produced under his supervision.[14] He was considered a master mechanic and developmental engineer, who served the Mack organization in various capacities until the time of his death.

Another veteran of the former Hewitt organization, who served the International Motor Company, was Maximilian C. Frins. He had started with Hewitt in 1906, serving as chief draftsman, first under E. R. Hewitt, and then under A. F. Masury.[15] In later years Max Frins continued his close collaboration with Masury, working out many engineering details on various Mack products.

By 1913 Hewitt and his old staff were apparently only involved with special equipment installations and truck service problems, due to the gradual phase-out of Hewitt truck production, which had continued on an ever decreasing scale at the 64th Street plant. But with the naming of E. R. Hewitt as chief engineer, an experienced team of master craftsmen would soon be at work again turning out superior truck designs, and creating legends in the process which would live long after them.

Changes and Compromises

In spite of the business recession which had restricted the overall growth of the motor truck industry during 1913, many new trends in truck design were taking place. These changes continued through 1914, having an important influence on most of the manufacturers.[16] One trend, which resulted in a strong selling point to those trucks adopting it, was worm-drive in place of the more traditional chain-drive. Worm-drive was a principal selling point of the heavy-duty Pierce-Arrow truck since its introduction in 1911. Another type of drive which increased in popularity after 1913 was double reduction, which had been used on the Autocar truck for several years. A third type of drive that came into vogue at this time was internal-gear, in which the final reduction was achieved through a gear ring inside of enlarged drums attached to the drive wheels.

A heavy-duty Mack Senior series dumper of 7-1/2 tons capacity hauling concrete for a 1913 construction project in New York City.

The manufacturers selecting worm, double reduction, or internal gear drive used the enclosed feature of these gearings as a claim for their superiority over chain-drive which, because of its obviously exposed operation, tended to be noisy. The comparative silence of the enclosed drives was called a proof of their efficiency. Mack engineers had their own opinion on this subject, and chain-drive would have its loyal adherents for many applications during several succeeding decades.

Another major trend that became evident during 1913 was the change in the position of the driver in relation to engine location.[17] The engine-under-floor design, (later called cab-over-engine) being so popular in America up to this point, was considered standard construction, especially on heavier truck models. On the other hand, the engine-in-front design was called the "European" type because so few foreign manufacturers built any other style. Mack had built both types since its entry into the motor truck market in 1905 but the lighter series Mack, Jr. line, introduced in 1909, was designed with engine in front. Even though the cab-over-engine truck had the advantage of a shorter turning radius, due to a shorter wheel base, and better weight distribution between front and rear axles, the easier engine accessibility

for servicing of the European type soon made this the dominant style in America, too.

The trend to left hand steering was also marked by 1914, with slightly over 50 per cent of the truck models offered at the beginning of the year having that design.[18] The switch in steering position was an important change, as it usually included the removal of the gearshift and parking brake levers from the exterior of the truck to the center of the cab floor, where they have basically remained ever since. Most Mack trucks and buses built up to this point had right hand steering, but as new models were designed they all were given the new left hand steering and center control features.

The use of governors on truck engines to protect them from the carelessness of some drivers had grown steadily since about 1912. Also, automatic advance on the timing of ignition systems had grown in popularity for the same reason. However, electric starting and lighting were still not popular features on trucks at this time due to a lack of demand on the part of the users, who largely viewed such refinements as costly and unnecessary extras.

A Senior series Mack with heavy wooden dump body and mechanical type under-body hoist.

Hauling rock from excavation for the Hotel Pennsylvania, New York City, in 1916. Note early steel dump body with Mack chain-hoist.

With these important changes in truck design taking place during 1913 and with the new line of monobloc-engined truck models now aborted, top management was no doubt anxious to see some new truck models introduced. This was especially true for the light and medium-duty lines where competition was gaining on the time-tested Mack designs. However, the firms's tight financial situation was still a major stumbling block to the development of new models, as there are indications that the board of directors did not wish to authorize funds to develop a new truck line whose major components would be manufactured in the company's plants. The directors might have reasoned that it would be less of a strain on capital to assemble trucks from components purchased from outside vendors than to invest in the costly retooling needed to make newly designed engines, transmissions, and rear axles.

When the proposal by the board of directors for the company to build only assembled trucks reached the operating level of management, the concept was strongly opposed.[19] There can be little doubt that Hewitt and his associates also challenged this concept, as they had never relied on outside engineers to design the parts that had gone into Hewitt trucks. In fact, E. R. Hewitt was known at this time for his outspoken ideas on automotive engineering, and his motor vehicles were considered quality products by all who knew them.

The result of the dispute between those wishing the firm to build "assembled" trucks and those sticking to the "manufactured" truck concept was an interesting compromise. Authorization was given for a line of medium-duty trucks to be designed with only the engine to be an "in-house" product, with most of the balance of the parts to be purchased from outside suppliers. This truck was to have a year's trial and, if successful, the engineering department would then be given carte blanche to go ahead with the design for a heavier series to be manufactured completely within the company's plants.[20]

Development of the Model AB Mack

It would have been out of character for E. R. Hewitt, master mechanic, engineer, metallurgist, and new chief engineer, to design an assembled truck made from "off-the-shelf" components without strong objections.[21] Hewitt and his staff quickly moved ahead with the designs for the new engine and basic specifications for the complete truck. A. F. Masury, who retained the title of service manager for several more months, no doubt began collaborating with Hewitt on the new truck design, using his valuable experience in observing the weak points of the hundreds of trucks which his department serviced. The new Mack model "AB," as it was named, turned out to be a smooth combination of Hewitt engineering concepts and some advanced commercial vehicle designs found only on a few European makes. A brief description of the AB model will indicate the direction that Mack engineering took under the new management.

In appearance the new AB Mack was quite modern looking for its time and marked the really first use of sheet metal for truck cab construction in the United States. A contemporary trade publication indicated a British influence in some of the design characteristics, and praised its appearance as being both utilitarian and substantial.[22] A streamlined effect was seen in the upward slope of the hood, which joined a neatly flared cowl. The cab itself was of all metal construction, having a flowing effect as it continued to widen behind the flared cowl. Horizontally sliding side doors, which disappeared when open were a standard feature, with a curved steel top being optional. This all metal cab construction was in sharp contrast to the open wooden seats with little or no protection against the elements, which passed for most truck cabs up to that time.

The AB engine had several unique features marking it apart from standard American designs, and which characterized Mack engines until the late 1920s. Large inspection ports, a feature of the earlier Hewitt engines, and a cross-shaft at the front for driving the magneto and water pump, were two outstanding features. The inspection ports had covers which could be quickly detached for the checking of wear to the connecting rod bearings, an important procedure which could not be followed on other engines without the time consuming steps of first unbolting and then dropping the oil pan. The crankshaft main bearings were of generous size, and all engine gears and shafts were heat treated for longer service life.

The use of the cross-shaft at the front of the engine for driving the magneto, which generated and timed the spark for ignition, was a means of overcoming a problem which apparently occurred sometimes with Hewitt trucks having the magneto drive parallel to the engine. In some instances, if a truck stopped with one front wheel much higher than the other, the twisting of the

frame would cause the engine to move out of alignment and also create a binding action in the magneto drive, thus making it impossible to start the truck until the front wheels were level again.[23] Some French cars and trucks, such as the Renault and De Dion - Bouton, had used the cross-shaft design quite successfully since the early 1900s. The AB engine had a bore and stroke of 4 x 5 inches, and was rated by the conservative S. A. E. formula at 25.6 hp. However, company literature truthfully stated that "on 100-hour continuous brake tests it averaged over 30 hp."

Another important feature of the AB engine was the incorporation of a centrifugal governor within the camshaft timing gear. The governor was completely enclosed, with the centrifugal weights activating the device being concealed in the camshaft timing gear. In effect, excessive engine speed acting on the weights caused a long rod, pushed by the weights, to close a butterfly valve in the throttle pipe and thereby hold the truck's speed to 16 miles per hour. This speed was considered the fastest a truck of the AB's capacity should go on solid rubber tires over the cobblestoned streets of the day. It was found that on pneumatic tires motor vehicles could usually double their speed without problems from excess vibration, but in 1914 practical pneumatic truck tires were still a few years in the future.

In keeping with the original construction concept the other major components were supplied by outside vendors. The Timken-Detroit Axle Company provided the worm-drive rear axle, much in vogue at the time. Left hand drive with steering gear supplied by the Gemmer Manufacturing Company, and center control with clutch and transmission provided by the Brown-Lipe

Gear Company, were also part of the original specifications.

The new model AB was introduced in record time, with the first deliveries being made by the fall of 1914, almost coinciding with the start of World War 1. It is believed that the first units may have had Continental[24] or Light engines, as the Hewitt designed power plants were apparently not ready yet. And at first, the AB models were built only with worm-drive at the Saurer plant in Plainfield, New Jersey, most likely because of a lack of production capacity at the Allentown factory where the Mack Seniors and Juniors with chain-drive were still being made. Apparently as production of the chain-drive Junior line was phased out during late 1915, model AB manufacture was then transferred to Allentown, and chain-drive was added as an option.

It was quite obvious to all concerned that the AB was a modern product in every respect, and the backlog of orders on the sales books soon proved this point. Before the expiration of the agreed upon trial year, the directors gave the go ahead to the new heavy-duty unit that was to be designed and built wholly within the organization.[25] However, a shift in management of the engineering department would bring to bear a unique personality on the future course of Mack product design.

Birth of the "Bulldog"

Evidently, Edward R. Hewitt felt quite restricted in his job as chief engineer and resigned the position, in his words, "...when I found I could not give the work the full attention required."[26] Another possible reason for his resignation can be found in one of Hewitt's autobiographical works, "...only designs which I made were manufactured. The new company should have been called the Hewitt Motor Company. But my friend Monel begged me not to insist on this, because so much money had been spent in advertising the Mack name, he said, and all this capital would be wasted if I insisted on having my name carried on the company's product."[27] But Hewitt did continue with the company as a consulting engineer for at least thirty years afterwards, making important contributions to many Mack engineering projects.

E. R. Hewitt's resignation took place at the end of June 1914, with his trusted associate, A. F. Masury, succeeding him as chief engineer.[28] A. H. Leipert, another close Hewitt associate, took over Masury's position as service manager. With the new AB project almost at the marketing stage, Masury could concentrate most of his efforts on the design of the new heavy-duty truck model that was so urgently needed to update the Mack line. Masury had evidently been also handling some of the larger fleet accounts in a sales function, along with his service operation, and he insisted on continuing to follow on these accounts as chief engineer. His argument was that in order to do a good job designing Mack trucks, he would have to be in close contact with representative users and he could think of no better way to keep such close contact than to handle their sales and service.[29]

Again, the engineering department prepared plans for the new model, to be called the AC, in record time. The directors gave their approval and final plans were drafted by November of 1914. It is interesting to note that E. R. Hewitt was now consulting engineer, while his former associate, A. F. Masury, was chief engineer. But there is no doubt both collaborated on the AC project, as they must have on the AB truck. Proof of their joint efforts are the patented features on AB and AC engines taken out in the names of either Hewitt, or Hewitt and Masury jointly. Other people certainly made contributions too, as Jack Winchester remembers advising on the radiator design for the AC by consulting his notes taken at the bus garage a couple of years before.[30]

As with the AB model a strong determination was evidenced for making the new AC Mack a modern and distinctive looking, as well as solidly built, truck. An all steel cab, with doors that slid out of sight vertically behind the running board aprons when opened, along with a dash mounted radiator and tapered hood, provided a design unlike anything on the road. The dashboard placement of the radiator was not actually a new concept at that time, as a number of trucks and cars also used this design. These vehicles usually had engine hoods which sloped down in front, and this style was generally referred to as being the Renault type hood, after the famous French motor vehicle which popularized its use. One of the first AC catalogs, published in 1916, referred to the hood as being, "...of the Renault type, designed to give a clear view of the road ..." Several different hood designs were actually tried, one with a more rounded frontal shape perhaps considered more stylish.

General specifications for the new model AC Mack included an enlarged version of the new Hewitt-Masury designed engine used in the AB. The AC had a bore and stroke of 5 x 6 inches, and was rated at 40 hp by the S. A. E. formula. As shown in an AC

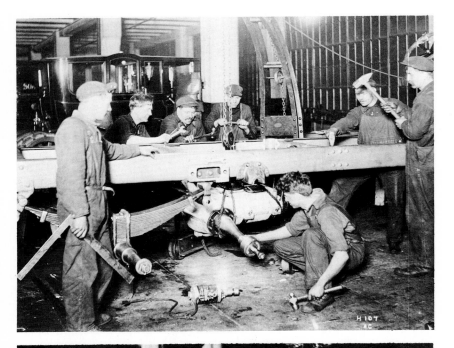

Aluminum was used for both the crankcase and oil pan of the AC engine. Note optional-extra starter, which was rarely specified for three-speed ACs.

Assembling the first prototype Model AC Mack at the 64th Street Plant, New York City, early in 1915.

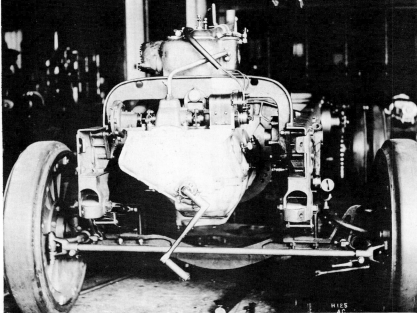

Direct front view of prototype AC with front cross-member removed. Note cradle-type suspension of engine, and tie rod in front of the axle.

Pair-cast cylinder blocks were a feature of all regular AC engines up to the late 1920s. Note inspection ports in crankcase.

The pressed steel cover and oil sump for the AC transmission could be easily removed to inspect the component without dropping it.

Housing for the three-speed transmission was made of cast aluminum. Note that transmission and jackshaft are combined in one unit.

catalog published a few years later, a brake horsepower rating of 74 at about 1,000 revolutions per minute, was the engine's actual power.

Patents had been granted on some of the engine's unique features, with the patent numbers being cast into the crankcases of both the AB and AC engines. Patent No. 1,135,524 covered the engine crankcase in which the ends of the crankcase were suspended by steel beams, using U-bolts running under the end bearings of the crankshaft for positive support. This patent was ostensibly to provide a means for detaching the lower portion of the crankcase without disturbing the crankshaft, but it also served to relieve the cast aluminum crankcase of most stresses while the engine was running. The front U-bolt extended up to a pivot arrangement with a steel cross-beam so that the engine's position could adjust to the distortion in the truck's frame, such as occurred when passing over a rough road.

The governor construction on the engine was covered by patent No. 1,148,318. The arrangement of the cross-shaft at the front of the engine for driving the magneto and water pump, was covered by patent No. 1,148,774. The patents covering the crankcase and governor construction were granted to E. R. Hewitt, and the patent on the cross-shaft to Messrs. Hewitt and Masury.

Final drive on the AC was by side chains driven from a jackshaft, which was constructed in one unit with a three-speed selective transmission. The old constant-mesh transmission previously used on Mack trucks was dispensed with due to the inclusion of a clutch brake with the single plate clutch, which helped to eliminate the clashing of gears when an inexperienced driver changed speeds. The new transmission had fewer moving parts, making for a more simplified design.

The foot, or service brakes were on the ends of the jackshaft between the driving sprockets and the frame side rails, while the hand, or parking brakes were located on the rear wheels. Through this design the driver's service braking effort was increased by the chain ratio between the driving and driven sprockets in the chain-drive system. And, should the chains fail for some extreme reason, the hand brakes could act positively on the rear wheels. The steering column was set at about a 45 degree angle with the frame, comparable with automobile design practice of the day. On the other hand, most trucks used a nearly 90 degree angle for setting their steering columns, which was almost straight up and down. The Mack engineers considered the 45 degree angle more comfortable and less tiring for the driver.

A pressed steel frame, heat treated for maximum resiliency, was another important feature of the AC, as it was a major change from the traditional use of the stiffer rolled steel frames on the Senior model Macks. Also, the side rails were straight from end to end, not tapered as with the smaller AB chassis, allowing the AC to have relatively heavy equipment secured to either end of its frame.

The IM (International Motor) monogram was used on the front of the hood, and was cast into major components and the radiator cap. Three basic tonnage capacities were offered: 3-1/2, 5-1/2, and 7-1/2, each in three standard wheel bases. There were also three comparable tractors in 7, 11, and 15-ton capacities. In short, the AC Mack's specifications called for a heavy-duty commercial vehicle having a unique design which balanced simplicity with strength, as well as offering a chassis adaptable to an extremely wide range of uses.

Testing the Prototypes

Two experimental test trucks were built at the 64th Street plant beginning in the winter of 1915. On one a large petroleum products tank was mounted, as this truck was destined for use in New Jersey as a "hot penetration" road oiler. It was evidently fully operational by the summer of 1915 and presented an impressive sight with the large tank, heater, and plumbing necessary to keep its load of hot asphalt ready for spreading. Adding to its utilitarian look were squared-off, military-type fenders, and a tapered hood with removable louvers. This prototype, (E-1?) of the soon to be famous AC received little or no publicity, but the other one, (E-2) did.

On Saturday, August 7, 1915, the Mack AC engineering test truck E-2 left New York City in a convoy of 15 motor vehicles headed for the U. S. Army training camp at Plattsburg, New York. Like the road oiler, the E-2 had military-type fenders, but the hood was rounded in front and had screening instead of louvers on the side. The big AC Mack, a 3-1/2 ton chassis, as well as a one-ton model AB, had been loaned to a new group of reserve officers organized as "the first motor gun troop in the country."[31] Traveling an average daily rate of 100 miles, the convoy reached Plattsburg on August 11th. In addition to pulling a standard three-inch field gun with caisson, the E-2 carried three rapid fire guns, thousands of rounds of ammunition, and 30 soldiers, for a total gross vehicle weight in excess of eight tons. Special demountable armor plating was attached to the sides of the body, and the E-2 was described as being practically a land gun boat.

The directors of the International Motor Company must have been quite pleased with the handiwork of the engineering department, as the AC was in full production at Allentown by January 1916. The Senior model Macks were phased out shortly thereafter, but production of Saurer trucks at Plainfield continued through 1917 due to a large influx of war orders. The First World War had helped to spur demand for trucks, and the AC found a ready market, soon proving itself a worthy successor to the old Mack and Hewitt heavy-duty models.

Prototype AC outside the 64th Street Plant with Chief Engineer A. F. Masury behind the wheel, and his assistant, Charles F. Drumm, alongside. Picture believed taken in March 1915.

Prototype AC shown taking on a load of hot asphalt before starting on a road paving job in New Jersey during the summer of 1915.

Another prototype AC was used to pull a three-inch field gun from New York City to Plattsburgh for an Army Reserve training encampment in August 1915.

The Mack AC was first introduced to the general public at the Boston Truck Show during the week of March 4th through 11th, 1916, and received many favorable comments in the trade press.[32] The hidden placement of the radiator was pointed to as an example of protecting a generally vulnerable component, as the tubes were placed behind steel screening which saved them from dislodgement in an accident. Another feature which was pointed to as being well thought out was the front chassis cross-member, which was actually a disguised bumper, bolted in place so that it could be quickly removed for full access to the lower front of the engine. The hood in its production version was squared-off, and had screening in the front and on the sides, a synthesis of the hoods used on the two prototypes in 1915.

Some truck operators who were aware of the development of the AC quickly placed orders, and before the spring of 1916 had

arrived sales had equalled expectations. The New Jersey based petroleum company which had tested one of the two prototypes quickly ordered a small fleet of AC's, and other orders were soon in hand from firms whose type of business would represent this Mack's chief market for many years after. Soon AC Macks were handling ice in the greater Boston area, coal in Baltimore, steel castings in Detroit, and milk, contractors' supplies, and general merchandise in New York.

The most significant as well as demanding market that the AC fitted was the grueling work of the general contractor. The Senior model Macks had long been popular among building contractors in many parts of the country, and in the large cities along the Eastern Seaboard there were few other makes of trucks in this service. Relative to the basic design of the AC, this significant statement appeared in a trade periodical: "...it is the opinion of the engineers responsible for the design that chain-drive is better adapted for the rigors of service with contractors and

First production AC unit, with Chassis Number 7001, was shipped to a Detroit castings company from the Allentown Plant on February 28, 1916. Note unusual type of cast steel wheels.

similar work for which these models are intended.''[33] This statement was a very accurate prophecy, for contractors were the most consistent buyers of chain-drive Macks, and many insisted on having this type of drive in their trucks long after the AC was superseded by more powerful models.

Even though a natural market in the heavy hauling field had been seen for the new AC, Masury continued to seek new markets for it by an endless series of experiments and demonstrations. Wrecker equipment was demonstrated on a stock chassis, resulting in sales to some cities as a heavy-duty tow truck for rescuing stranded or damaged fire apparatus. Other municipal uses were as a street flusher and garbage truck, and several early sales of these were registered in New York. The ingenuity of Masury and his staff in demonstrating the versatility of the Mack AC resulted in its achieving a far wider degree of sales penetration than any other heavy-duty truck marketed in America.

The Bulldog Earns His Name

It was thought to be a conflict of limited duration when it burst forth early in August 1914, but as the months passed the European War kept taking on the dimensions of what would later be called the Great War and the "war to end all wars." By 1916 six of Europe's greatest countries were involved: England, France, Germany, Italy, Russia, and the old Austro-Hungarian Empire, made up of several diverse national groups. Resources of the combatants were being used to the utmost and American factories were soon backlogged with orders from its traditional trading partners, England and France.

Later observers of the World War considered motor transport as a vital factor in deciding the outcome in favor of the Allied side. Two outstanding examples of motor transport saving an extremely grave military situation for the Allied side were the Battle of the Marne, fought in the fall of 1914, and the Siege of Verdun, a protracted struggle early in 1916. In the first instance the Paris Garrison was rushed to the Marne River, by taxis, buses, trucks, and private autos, just in time to stem a German advance aimed at the capture of the French Capital. If successful, it might have forced a very unfavorable settlement on the French.

After the relative stabilization of the battle lines in Northern France many sectors of the front could only be supplied by motor vehicles, although light railway networks were set up at certain

Early 1916 AC used by a Boston area ice company. Rounded crown-type fenders, straight-peaked cab, and finely meshed hood screening, were features of only the first month's production units it is thought.

Rounded AC hoods may have looked more fashionable in 1916, but they lacked the rugged character of the squared-off design that was quickly adopted for regular production units.

This 1917—1918 AC army transport truck was most likely built as a demonstration unit for obtaining government orders. Note plain seat box, and the louvers which replaced the hood screening during 1917.

The 1917 Bulldog army transport truck featured special bumper, dual ignition, and extra piping connections for the cooling system.

points by both sides. It is believed that the British had upwards of 1,000 buses in service transferring soldiers from one sector to another as the fighting ebbed and flowed.

In the early months of 1916, the French city of Verdun became the focal point for a German campaign whose purpose was to destroy its local fortifications and open a way to Paris from the east. With no adequate railways in the area large fleets of military transport trucks were pressed into service, continuing to supply the vital bastion until the German offensive finally failed.[34] Many of the trucks used to save Verdun were supplied by American manufacturers, and by 1916 both Britain and France had become dependent on America to supply a vital portion of the transportation needs of their military forces.

Early in 1917 a British purchasing mission visited one of the Mack plants to inspect the Model AC and the firm's production capabilities, and ordered 150 after being satisfied that it was a quality product and suitable for their needs. It was reported in a trade magazine that, "In appearance these Macks, with their pugnacious front and resolute lines, suggest the tenacious quality of the British Bull Dog. In fact, these trucks have been dubbed 'Bull Dog Macks' by the British engineers in charge."[35] A company executive, perhaps Masury himself, accompanying the British delegation must have been so struck by the analogy of the AC to the staunch English canine, that the truck's nickname was quickly accepted by Mack management. The spelling of "Bulldog" in reference to the model AC was continued as two words until sometime in the late 1920s.

The origin and tradition of the English bulldog goes back hundreds of years. Bull-baiting might be called the English version of the Spanish bullfight, and most likely had its height of popularity several hundred years ago, when even Queen Elizabeth was believed to have attended such contests.[36] In the sport of bull baiting, a canine, man's best friend, instead of a human, faced a bull, and it was the dog's job to seize the bull with his teeth and to hold on for as long as possible. These events were naturally won by the dogs showing the greatest tenacity, and, it should be added, the stakes were sometimes very high with much money won or lost on a favored dog. The bulldog was therefore the result of breeding a canine that had not only the strength of bite and the tenacity to hold onto an adversary many times his size, but also the uncommon courage to tackle such a challenge!

Several months after the British order, a large government contract was signed in November 1917, which called for a minimum purchase of 900 "Bull Dog" trucks for the U. S. Army Corps of Engineers. The initial order totaled over $4 million and called for only the heaviest Macks, the 5-1/2 and 7-1/2 ton versions of the model AC.[37] At that time Mack production was at a rate of 260 trucks a month, and the Allentown plant facilities had to be quickly enlarged to meet the growing business.

After America's declaration of war in April 1917, U. S. doughboys started arriving in France the following June under the command of General John F. "Black Jack" Pershing. To the "Engineers" fell the monumental task of building fortifications, hospitals, and barracks, and maintaining the vital railway and highway links in the war zone, for the two million men of the American Expeditionary Forces who eventually got "over there."

The Bulldog Macks which reached France were used for almost every conceivable haulage task since the job of the Engineers was so diverse and all encompassing. During wartime the job of the U. S. Army Corps of Engineers is basically twofold: the construction of military installations and the building and maintaining of vital transportation links behind the front lines. The following names of the Engineering regiments involved will give a more precise idea of the scope of the Corps undertaking: Water-Supply, Highways, Light-Railroading, Standard-Gauge

Finished Bulldogs await delivery to the Army Corps of Engineers, at Allentown, during the summer of 1918.

Helping to build all-weather roads at U.S. Army base camps in France was an important assignment for the Bulldogs belonging to the "Engineers."

The Bulldogs of Motor Transport Company No. 695 have their hoods raised for morning inspection at Lormont, France, on May 11, 1919.

Railroading, Gas and Flame, Forestry, Mining, Quarrying, General Construction, Engineers' Supplies, and Surveying.[38] In addition to these duties the Engineers had a close support role to other sectors of the army, such as the development of camouflage and searchlight defenses.

Many Bulldogs were equipped with dump bodies for hauling sand and gravel to the many construction sites. Others had simple flat bed, general cargo, or special bodies, depending upon the type of service for which the trucks were intended. One group of AC's had double radiators and a 25 KW generator driven by the engine to supply electricity for two huge mobile searchlights, which were transported in the bodies of the trucks. A total of 4,470 Bulldogs, including some of the 3-1/2 tonners, were eventually bought for the Engineers, with 1,586 of these being received in France by December 1, 1918.[39]

The army Bulldogs did such an outstanding job of delivering the goods that their reputation became a legend among the doughboys who had seen them in action. It was generally acknowledged that the Mack AC was so solidly put together that it would take abuse from rough service that was "above and beyond the call of duty." Because of their outstanding service

one trade paper suggested some national recognition in an editorial:[40]

Behind the fighting lines, "over there," many squadrons of Mack trucks were in constant use, in the building and repairing of roads, the hauling of guns, the speeding of supplies of all sorts through shell holes, waste fields, snow and ice and every imaginable hard condition - all this varied and fine performance stamps with an indelible impress the Mack truck as a winner just as surely as the armistice proclaimed the victory of our armies, of which it was and is a part.

The Bulldog Serves the Home Front

No less important to American's war effort were the industrial activities on the home front, and the transportation network, made up of rails, roads, and waterways through which flowed the output of farm and factory. The ever increasing burden placed upon the railroads had a telling effect by 1916, with shortages of various types of freight cars becoming common. Even with the desire and increased financial ability to improve their services the railroad situation seemed only to grow worse, especially after America's direct entry into the war. Car shortages and congestion at terminals became a prime concern to Federal authorities whose responsibilities were to see the A. E. F., as well

as other Allied armies, supplied with as much munitions and equipment as possible so that the war could be brought to a speedy conclusion. By presidential proclamation, in December 1917 the Federal government took over the American railroads in order to pool their resources and move traffic over the shortest routes possible.[41]

Owners of motor trucks had already been proving the old axiom that necessity is the mother of invention. When railroad freight cars could not be obtained for the delivery of their new vehicles by the factory, many purchasers sent drivers to bring them back overland. Such "drive-aways" became quite common in 1917 and 1918, with distances of up to several hundred miles being driven in convoys or by single vehicles. Since there were few paved roads outside of most major cities at that time, it took nerve to even contemplate such travel. However, while the feasibility of drive-aways was proven quite practical, the movement of freight by motor truck between distant cities was attempted on a more limited scale.

In the spring of 1916 a fleet of five model AC Macks, some pulling full trailers, made a run of 140 miles from New York City to Hartford, Connecticut, with a 44 ton load of steel ball bearings.[42] The ball bearings were vitally needed by the S. K. F. Ball Bearing Company, a Swedish concern which had established a branch factory in the United States, but was still importing some materials. While overland runs of about 100 miles by some truckers was not considered too unusual in the East, where the roads tended to be kept open most of the year, the poorer road conditions in many other parts of the country made such trips extremely difficult if not impossible.

The most ambitious and well publicized of the attempts to beat the railroad blockade through the use of motor trucks was undertaken in the spring of 1917 by the Goodyear Tire and Rubber Company. The route was 740 miles in length, from Akron, Ohio, to Boston, Massachusetts, and by the end of the year the Goodyear fleet of seven trucks included a Bulldog Mack.[43] All the trucks, which included Packards and Whites, were equipped with huge pneumatic tires, and the trips were undertaken as much to demonstrate the practicality of the tires as to haul Goodyear rubber products to Boston and tire fabric back to the Akron plant. Actually, the long overland runs which took the trucks over the

Allegheny Mountains in all kinds of weather, would have been almost impossible had the trucks not used pneumatic tires. Not only would the trips have taken twice as long, losing much of the value involved, but the trucks would have shown the strains from the uneven roads much sooner if they had been equipped with solid rubber tires.

The 3-1/2 ton Bulldog truck used on the Akron to Boston run had some unusual design features. The body, which was of the removable rack type, had a steel sleeping compartment located above and to the rear of the cab. Since the trucks were operated on a 24 hour schedule it was found desirable for two drivers to accompany each run, and it may very well be that the Goodyear operation introduced the sleeper compartment concept to over-the-road trucking. High speed was another important feature of the Goodyear Mack, which was designed to average between 30 and 35 miles per hour while using large driving sprockets. A set of smaller jackshaft sprockets was carried for negotiating heavy grades.[44] The tires mounted single front and rear were quite large, being 38 x 7 inches on the front wheels and 44 x 10 on the rear.

A fine showing was made by the Goodyear Bulldog during the early winter of 1918. In spite of heavy snow conditions, especially in the mountainous sections of Pennsylvania, and sub-zero temperatures, the Mack AC made a 533 mile run between New York and Akron in 49 hours actual running time.[45]

Other concepts of motor truck use were popularized during the 1917 to 1918 period to help lick America's transportation crisis. The use of semi-trailers pulled by short wheel-based truck tractors was a method of increasing the total payload a single driver could deliver, since the tractor, functioning mainly as a power unit, carried part of the load with the trailer axle carrying the rest of the weight. The use of semi- and full-trailers sped up the turn around time of each unit, with the drivers able to pickup loaded trailers rather than having to wait to have their trucks filled with cargo. The Bulldog Mack was especially adapted for use as a truck-tractor. It was originally sold with a unique company designed fifth wheel device, popularly known as the "Waffle-Iron Fifth Wheel," for providing the flexible connection between the tractor and trailer.

Many of the original tractor-trailer combinations were simply heavy horse-drawn wagons with the front running gear removed and a matching device for the tractor's fifth wheel substituted. Common conversions of this type were made in the dairy, coal,

Tractor versions of the Model AC were available right from 1916. Here a 1919 Bulldog pulls a heavy semi-trailer used for carrying milk to a local distribution plant.

Early semi-trailers lacked landing gear and the coupling process was, therefore, quite tedious. Note heavy wooden construction of trailer and simple design of fifth wheel.

and lumber businesses, and in fire departments. However, the First World War period spurred the growth of specialized trailer builders, who soon broke from the old wagon building practices of large diameter steel-tired wheels, and were making automotive type trailers having rubber-tired truck wheels by 1919.

Progress on Many Fronts

The end of World War I in November 1918 found the name and fame of the Mack truck soaring to new highs of public recognition. The large government orders as well as civilian demand had created severe strains on the Mack plants, which had to be enlarged several times during the late war period. A new prosperity had also been a needed result of all the company's activities, and these funds were wisely used to hire additional engineers and skilled workers, push experimental work, and obtain additional plant facilities for the postwar boom period.

During the three year period, 1917 through 1919, the engineering staff of the International Motor Company embarked upon a number of important engineering studies. The three basic truck components: engines, transmissions, and final drives, were studied in depth with a number of patents developed for each. This work was done at the New York headquarters building on 64th Street, and was in addition to the war work and special equipment installations that were a regular part of the Mack business at that time.

Experimental work on a new truck engine centered around one designed to avoid the use of heavy castings by employing pressed steel. The new four-cylinder engine was water-cooled, with the water jacket surrounding the cylinders constructed integrally with a barrel-type crankcase, all formed from folded and welded sheet steel. The short two-bearing crankshaft was mounted on plain bearings. Overhead valves were used, which operated by bevel gears connected to the crankshaft through an exposed front shaft with two rubber-impregnated fabric U-joints.[46] This engine was installed in the 1919 E-15 test truck,

The E-15 test truck used the experimental Model AD welded sheet metal engine, and had bevel gear drive rear axle.

The experimental 1918 Bulldog chassis was no doubt inspired by the advent of major development work on pneumatics by the tire industry.

The large differential housing on top of the rear axle indicates a dual reduction drive. Note also the parking brake mounted on the propeller shaft, just behind the transmission.

Extra cooling capacity was needed for the pneumatic-tired Bulldog because of continuous power output required to sustain high speed operation. Note large tank on top of engine with piping going back to the radiator.

Various experimental Model ACs and ABs were tested at the end of W. W. I, mainly to get data on different types of rear end drives.

which resembled the Bulldog in hood design and radiator placement. However, the E-15 had an exposed radiator, a flywheel blower for cooling, and a special transmission arrangement for a straight line drive to a single reduction bevel rear axle.

During 1918 the company produced a prototype Bulldog with large pneumatic tires mounted on steel spoked wheels and having a special double reduction rear axle. This truck had an auxiliary water tank for the radiator, as high speed use of the basically slow speed AC engine no doubt could have caused an over-heating problem at times.

The question of worm or other enclosed final drives versus chain drive seemed to have been settled by all the major truck manufacturers except Mack by 1919. Masury was still not satisfied that worm-drive was the answer, although it had become the dominant type of rear axle for heavy-duty trucks. Several Bulldog trucks were equipped with worm-drive and other types of geared axles, and driven around the countryside to test their efficiency. According to company records as many as 30 worm-drive 5-1/2 ton Bulldog trucks may have been built in 1919 for customers wishing that form of drive. Records also show that about a dozen Bulldogs with double reduction were produced about the same time.

With an improved financial situation helping, the directors of the International Motor Company decided on a plan to reorganize the firm's corporate structure. On November 8, 1916, the Interna-

tional Motor Truck Corporation was incorporated as a holding company for the operating arm of the overall organization, which included manufacturing and sales subsidiaries. Sales of $11.7 million were recorded in 1917, resulting in a net profit of $1.1 million.[47]

Mack management was strengthened by the naming of Alfred J. Brosseau to head the company in 1917.[48] A. J. Brosseau was formerly head of the Federal Motor Truck Company and had many years of experience in both the truck and farm equipment industries. Robert E. Fulton, an early promoter of the Saurer truck, had become sales manager by this time and he worked very closely with Chief Engineer Masury to maximize public recognition of all Mack products. Many returning servicemen were hired by the company, and several outstanding personalities started long careers with Mack at this time. By 1919 Masury had been made an official, being elected a vice-president of the International Motor Company in recognition of his value to the organization. Sales of $22.1 million in 1919 were almost double those of 1917, and resulted in a net profit of almost $2 million.[49]

By 1919 a national advertising campaign was fully under way to further popularize the Bulldog Mack. Even the AC Macks purchased by the army kept adding to the company's prestige through their display in victory parades and special exhibitions. New York City's Fifth Avenue was the stage for a huge mobile war pageant on Saturday, May 3, 1919, which took four hours to pass by any one point. A contemporary newspaper account[50] called it, "...the mightiest military spectacle ever staged," and it was officially called "The Panorama of Victory." Many army Bulldogs were used as floating displays to show everything from military support equipment to sand bag entrenchments and barbed wire entanglements. Another display of army equipment and captured German military machines was held later in the year at a New York City armory.[51]

Also in 1919, the War Department decided to put on a national demonstration billed as the First Transcontinental Army Convoy. A total of 72 vehicles, mostly trucks, made the two month trip from Washington, D.C., to San Francisco during the middle of the summer. Many Bulldogs were included in the convoy, some with machine shop equipment and others with bridging devices and important supplies. As a young staff officer, Dwight D. Eisenhower was on this trip, and later recounted some of its adventures in one of his memoirs.[52]

Army Bulldogs were one of the star attractions in many patriotic parades following the Armistice on November 11, 1918. Here a group of ACs, carrying Whippet tanks, parade up New York's Fifth Avenue on Army Day 1930.

A float in the huge military parade held in New York on May 3, 1919, called The Panorama of Victory. Many doughboys slept in such dugouts while fighting at the front.

Bulldog searchlight truck and searchlight unit at special exhibit of military hardware held in New York City. Extra radiator was needed for the Bulldog because of the stationary use of the engine.

Part of the First Transcontinental Army Convoy kicking up dust clouds in the arid wastes of Wyoming during the summer of 1919.

If nothing else, the convoy's struggles with weak bridges and almost nonexistent roads focused attention of government officials and the public alike on the need for national highways. But with the doughboys streaming back from Europe, longing to return to civilian life, the public would want to forget the Great War and return to the process of building America. The call for a "return to normalcy" would soon be a popular political rallying cry.

The Mack chain hoist required a special cab for the AC. Note lack of vertical sliding doors and lower skirting.

Fitted out as a winch-truck, the AC demonstrates its potential ability as an automotive wrecker. Note use of chain-guard to keep out dust and to muffle chain noise.

Loading several tons of artifical stone on 1917 AC. Over-head hoist was fabricated by the Hendrickson Motor Truck Co., Chicago.

A huge steel fabrication for the base of a solar telescope project provided a 200% overload for this Model AC before its epic struggle up Mt. Wilson, California, in 1916. Jack Stoner, Southern California agent for Mack, stands looking up at the left.

This 1918 solid-tired Bulldog followed a regular route between New York and Philadelphia, helping shippers beat the railroad bottleneck of World War I.

A 1917 pneumatic-tired Bulldog used by the Goodyear Tire and Rubber Company to demonstrate the practicality of pneumatics in motor truck service. Note sleeping compartment with sliding window, behind cab, used by either of the two drivers needed for the truck's overland trips.

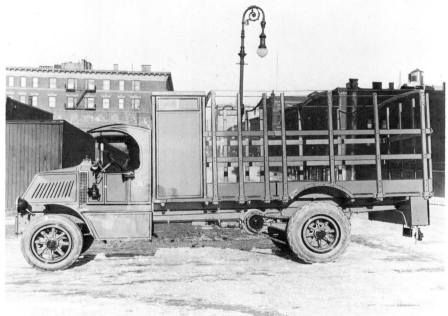

Long Branch, New Jersey, acquired this AC city service ladder early in 1919. Photo taken outside plant of Utica, New York, firm making final installation of the equipment.

Chicago Fire Dept. using a 1917 AC tractor to pull a 65 foot aerial ladder.

Dumping refuse at a landfill site using the Mack chain hoist. Note improved sanitary method of transporting waste material through the use of enclosed dump body.

Waste collection was a slow and unsanitary process before the AC. Note small rear wheels to lower body height in order to ease labor of loading.

Fleet of 1916 AC's built earlier that year. Patriotic posters on bodies advocate the sending of packages "To the boys at the front," no doubt referring to the Mexican Campaign of 1916.

U.S. Navy NC-4 Curtiss seaplane refueling on the Ohio River at Louisville after its famous trans-Atlantic flight in 1919.

Use of full-trailers saved man power during World War I. Here a driver and his helper are managing a double cargo with the aid of a 1916 AC.

A Bulldog hay ride helps to bring a "return to normalcy" feeling to these people on a summer evening in Knoxville, Tennessee. John C. Rowold, later a veteran Mack sales executive, is seated on the running board.

Trucking in the Early Twenties

The early 1920s were exciting times in the motor truck industry, and the Bulldog Mack not only shared in the excitement, but also made much of its own.

The pace of the national economy had been greatly accelerated by the need to meet war-time production goals. With the war now over and many businesses having the funds, or credit, available with which to acquire speedier processes, it was inevitable that the demand for motor trucks would grow apace. The horse really began to lose ground rapidly in the early 1920s, with total truck sales reaching 321,789 in 1920, as compared to 92,130 in 1916,[1] the first full year of Bulldog truck production.

Adding zest to the rapidly rising demand among the more conventional users were the new or expanding fields where the heavy-duty truck was also proving its worth. Although over-the-road trucking was still in its earliest stages, Bulldog Macks, in both tractor and straight truck versions, were proving quite popular. Highway trucking was mainly over the better roads connecting nearby cities in the more industrialized parts of the country, and was an attempt to regularize a service that was mainly started as a stopgap during the railroad car shortage of World War I.

Truck use in the mining and lumbering industries was found to be more efficient than previous methods. Heretofore, temporary railroad tracks had often been laid, only to be shifted as operations dictated. Also, horses and mules had been used in many areas, and it was finally realized by more and more operators that beasts of burden could not keep up with the pace of modern industry. Bulldogs were soon hauling huge logs out of the forests of Washington and Oregon, and granite from the quarries of Vermont and New Hampshire.

Road building took on huge proportions during the early 1920s, having received its big push from the Federal Aid Road Act

A lusty war record behind it, the Bulldog came on strong during the Roaring Twenties. A painted outdoor advertisement in the Minneapolis area shortly after World War I.

This Bulldog rig, with early refrigerated semi-trailer built from AC components, started serving the Dallas-Ft. Worth area in 1922.

Hauling out heavy timber by three-speed Bulldog in Washington State.

Snowplowing was a second, but vital, duty for this street flusher. Based on the Bulldog's dependability and versatility, demand expanded greatly and Mack's Public Works Department was created in the early 1920s to handle municipal sales.

Akron, Ohio, used its AC to pull as many as six refuse filled full-trailers to the dump site, nine miles outside the city.

of 1916. The Federal Highway Act of 1921 added funds of $200 million to help finish the inter-state trunk line system originated in 1916 with an appropriation of $75 million. The Lincoln Highway was the object of most of the Federal involvement at this time, but many states were also adding their own road building projects to the rapidly expanding national highway network. Heavy-duty trucks, many of them Bulldogs, participated in this construction work, which continued with little pause throughout the Roaring Twenties.

While the "Good Roads Movement" dated back many years, its real impetus came with the mass production of the automobile and the consequent clamor from all classes of users for better road networks. As the public gradually depended more and more on automobiles for year-round service, the concept of

all-weather roads grew, and the elimination of the deeply rutted ones became essential.

The "Ship by Truck" movement, sponsored by the Firestone Tire and Rubber Company in 1920, also helped to focus attention on the need for better roads. Like the Goodyear Wingfoot Express promotion of the use of pneumatic truck tires in the late World War I period, the Firestone campaign of the early 1920s was aimed at the commercial shipper. It promoted both the use of motor trucks, and the good roads movement as a necessary concomitant.

Municipal services were a prime and growing market for the model AC Mack. The Bulldog's use in sanitation, road maintenance, and fire protection was extended with the adoption of auxiliary equipment. Akron, Ohio, used an AC as a truck-tractor to pull as many as six four-wheel dump trailers to a garbage disposal site nine miles outside the city limits.[2]

First introduced in 1919, a new fire pumper quickly established a fine reputation for dependability with the Chicago

Fire Department, which purchased five identical units by 1920. The new Bulldog pumper had a specially designed Northern rotary pump of 500 gallons per minute rated capacity. Mack AC's were also used as tractors to pull aerial ladders, which had been previously horse-drawn. The City of Baltimore purchased at least 20 World War I war surplus AC Macks and had various types of fire fighting equipment installed on them. Some of these World War I Bulldogs were still in service in the early 1970s with the Baltimore Fire Department.[3]

Heavy hauling in the urban centers of the country was still the Bulldog's forte, with the construction, fuel, and general trucking fields being the main users. The construction industry continued as one of the AC's best customers, with both excavating contractors and building supply houses usually favoring for their work the chain-drive and high engine torque at low revolutions-per-minute features. These features were considered by many to be essential in enabling a truck to get in and out of rugged construction sites.

Bulldog fire apparatus fighting a big city fire in the mid-1920s. Note water tower used to effectively aim water stream through the upper-story window of the burning warehouse.

One of six combination pumper and hose wagons purchased by Chicago during 1919 and 1920. This style of apparatus was called a Type AC-2.

This Type AC-6 fire apparatus tractor, with Sewell cushion wheels, was delivered to the City of Minneapolis in 1920.

The Type AC-3, combination pumper, chemical, and hose wagon, proved a popular style of fire apparatus for many departments during the 1920s. This one belonged to Plymouth, Pennsylvania.

Coal merchants were also growing Bulldog fleet owners, as their trucks were basically dump trucks with the high capacity bodies necessary for the efficient delivery of coal to large urban users. The Mack AC's straight heavy frame construction made it ideal for dump truck service. Heavy hauling contractors, who carried everything from general merchandise to newsprint paper, liked the AC's efficiency in carrying both extra-heavy loads at low speeds and lighter burdens at comparatively higher speeds. The jackshaft driving sprockets could be changed to suit different service requirements, although few owners are believed to have bothered to make this change. However, this ability to change the rearend gear ratios was a good selling point, as there were five

Taking on a load of sand with the aid of a mechanical loader.
Note hood hatch opened slightly to provide the Bulldog with
some additional cool air.

A group of three-speed Bulldogs hauling dirt from a foundation
excavation in Fresno, California, about 1924.

A dumper, with special cab and Mack chain-hoist, pulling out of a deep excavation for an office building on Madison Avenue, New York City, in 1920.

Bulldog coal truck with high capacity body and mechanical hoist. The Bulldog nameplate appeared on the sides of Mack cabs late in 1921.

High-lift bodies were common in the coal delivery field in some cities, where extended chutes were necessary to help deliver coal by gravity across wide sidewalks.

A future Mack truck driver gets some stimulation by holding the wheel of this Chicago-based Bulldog. Note Dayton cast steel wheels which came into vogue in the early 1920s.

A tanker serving a petroleum bulk station in Connecticut about 1921.

Templar sport touring car offers an interesting contrast to the large 1920 Bulldog tanker used to supply lubricants to an automobile racing team.

This 1920 AC was equipped with a Davis 1,000 gallon, two-compartment, petroleum tank, and is believed to be the first Bulldog shipped to Australia.

optional jackshaft sprocket sizes in addition to the one supplied on a given chassis.

Less demanding, although still considered in the heavy service catagory, were the loads trucked by the larger wholesale food houses. The delivery of canned foods, bottled drinks, as well as crated fresh vegtables, could be economically delivered to stores and institutions in lots weighing several tons. Flour in sacks weighing about 100 pounds each was often delivered to both the small neighborhood baker and large commercial bakery in Bulldog Macks. The only flat note during this period was the passage by Congress of the Volstead Act, in October 1919, which virtually closed every brewery in the United States in 1920, depriving the Bulldog Mack of one of its growing markets.

Some resentment to the use of both automobiles and motor trucks had been voiced by certain sectors of the public right from the dawn of the auto age. Most of the complaints came from drivers of horse-drawn vehicles, whose animals shied from the noisy metal monsters. However, as the automobile became an accepted means of transportation by World War I, motor trucks then became the target for restrictive legislation. The major complaint, which followed the growing use of trucks during the war period, was that they were responsible for damaging the roads in some areas. By 1919 some states had enacted laws which limited the capacity of motor vehicles to five tons. Mack engineers had the job of modifying their truck designs so that owners of new Macks could haul the maximum amount of payload while complying with some new state gross vehicle weight laws.

Early in 1920, Mack announced the introduction of a 6-1/2 ton Bulldog, replacing the 5-1/2 ton model. At the same time it was also stated that the capacity of the former 5-1/2 tonner was modified to five tons. Tractor models were also available in 10 and 13 ton capacities, corresponding to the new five and 6-1/2 ton

Delivering groceries to one of 400 outlets owned by a large Brooklyn-based chain-store operation early in 1922. Note the articulation of tractor and semi-trailer permits convenient unloading without the blockage of street traffic.

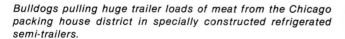

Bulldogs pulling huge trailer loads of meat from the Chicago packing house district in specially constructed refrigerated semi-trailers.

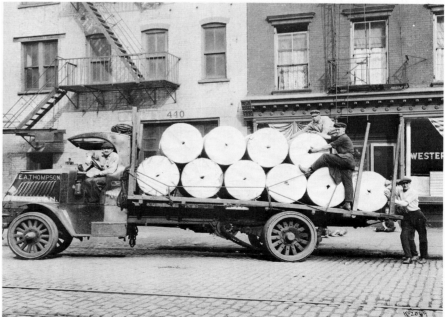

Newsprint rolls provide a capacity load for this 1920 Bulldog.

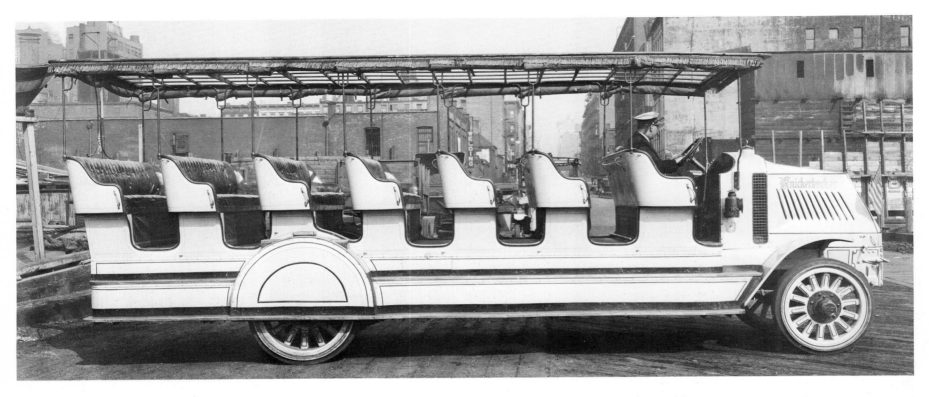

Sightseeing bodies of the 1920s provided few obstructions to the view of the passengers, but, on the other hand, also little protection in case of sudden downpours.

The sightseeing industry was a pioneer user of Mack buses. Here a New York operator displays a 1919 and two 1916 Bulldogs.

One of several Bulldog buses owned by a Plainfield, New Jersey, operator after World War I. Note use of large shock absorbers in place of front spring shackles and Sewell cushion wheels to help smooth the ride for passengers.

models. The overall width of the new Bulldogs was just under 90 inches, a reduction of about one inch, also to comply with the new state motor vehicle laws.[4] However, chassis number records indicate that some 5-1/2 ton Bulldogs were built after 1920, and that a few with five ton capacity had been built as early as 1918.

A few other modifications to the original production Bulldogs had taken place by 1920 that are worthy of note. The first obvious change occurred in 1917, with the substitution of 11 louvers for the former screening on either side of the engine hood. A hood-hatch to provide additional cooling was incorporated in the top of the hood during 1919. At the end of 1919, a high-tension Aero magneto with automatic impulse starting device was substituted for the combination of magneto, auxiliary vibrating coil, and battery formerly supplied as standard ignition. Most owners of AC's used either kerosene oil, acetylene gas, or a combination of the two for lighting their trucks. In most cases tail lights used kerosene, as did side lights. Acetylene was used for headlights and sometimes for tail lights. Electricity, when used, was for headlights, side lights, and tail lights.

Some New Concepts in Product Design

The International Motor Company's headquarters building on West 64th Street must have been the scene of feverish activity during 1919 and 1920. Several new prototype vehicles were

engineered, built up, tested, and a series of experiments begun which led quickly to the development of a revolutionary new system of rubber-block chassis vibration insulators. All this work was in addition to the company's regular output, the demand for which had continued to boom after World War I. The engineering staff was strengthened further with some top talent which had been released from the military service during 1919 and 1920. Also, the scale of the experiments necessitated the use of both the Allentown and Plainfield plants.

Work went forward during 1920 on the testing of the welded sheet metal engine, which had been first tried in the 1919 E-15 engineering test truck. The new concept in engine construction seemed to offer an attractive possibility for Mack to produce a comparatively light weight power plant on a mass production basis. According to engineering notes, the four-cylinder engine, while having only two main bearings, developed its optimum horsepower at 3,000 rpm with little or no vibration. The 3-3/4 inch bore by 5-3/4 inch stroke indicated a nominal horsepower rating similar to the AB engine, but the much higher rpm indicate at least a 50 brake horsepower rating.

Since the engine held much promise for successful development it was given the model designation AD, as was the E-15 test Truck, and a similar engine was installed in at least one other experimental vehicle. The prototype AF truck, completed in 1920, was similar in outer design to the E-15. A familiar Bulldog hood enclosed the AD engine and the improved cooling system, first used on the E-15, was also incorporated in the design. The AF radiator differed from the contemporary AC radiator in being straight sided and exposed to ambient air, rather than semicircular and hidden by screening. It is believed that the AF had a flywheel mounted blower instead of the usual AC-type belt-driven fan. Also, a new dual reduction axle was installed at the rear, and all four wheels had pneumatic tires, being 36 x 6 singles in front and 42 x 9 singles at the rear.

The AF Mack was a snappy looking truck with the "AF" model designation painted on the rear wheel hubs. From the finished appearance of the prototype, it could be assumed that the new model was just a step or two from actual production. However, it has been reported that welding difficulties, necessitating the expenditure of additional time and money, caused the abandonment of the basic engine project.[5] Actually, by the fall of 1920 a postwar economic recession had hit the country, effecting adversely the sales and profits of most commercial enterprises. Truck sales were especially hard hit, with 1921 seeing a reduction of 50 percent in factory sales as compared with 1920.[6] It followed that many firms had to restrict their engineering budget to only the most promising projects, due to a big reduction in their cash-flow.

Despite the shelving of the AD engine project and its companion truck models, the AD with bevel gear drive and the AF with dual reduction drive, new components for improved AB and AC Macks were soon a very positive result. Briefly stated, the "Tin Motor," as it was later referred to by company personnel, evidently required welding techniques and metallurgical knowledge far in advance of the state of the art in 1920. Experimental work on a sheet metal engine was taken up again by the Mack engineers in the 1930s and 1940s, but again with indifferent results. Mack engineers filing for patents on the original engine designs were Gus Leipert, A. F. Masury, and A. G. Herreshoff.[7]

The announcement, in January 1921, that worm-drive would be dropped in the model AB truck, stated that the new dual reduction rear axle replacing the worm had been under development for five years.[8] There certainly was no secret that the Mack engineers were not satisfied with the efficiency of the worm-drive axle and had been testing other types of gears. The new axle was really an outstanding engineering development, being used on various successive medium-duty, and later heavy-duty Mack

Front view of the 1920 AF shows the new exposed radiator design that would soon be adopted for the Model AC.

The prototype AF model provided the vehicle for testing several new components, such as the new Mack dual reduction rear axle. Note the unusual mounting and ramp for the two different size spare tires.

vehicles for many years. Also introduced on the improved AB was a company designed and manufactured unit clutch and transmission, replacing the vendor built component supplied since 1914.

The concept of a six-wheel motor vehicle was slowly gathering interest in commercial vehicle circles, partly as a means to ease the weight restrictions placed on the axles of heavy trucks by certain states. Spreading the vehicle's load over six instead of four wheels not only helped to ease the impact on the road, it was also considered a practical way of putting heavy-duty trucks on pneumatic tires. Mack engineers did some preliminary design work in this area as early as 1921, but it is doubtful if any six-wheeled Mack trucks were built until 1923.

By 1923 strong interest was being shown in a six-wheeled motor bus, most likely because of the better riding quality provided by the extra set of rear wheels. During 1924 an experimental six-wheel motor bus, named the Mack Greatcoach was completed and shown to various bus operators. The Greatcoach was apparently powered by the experimental AJ six-cylinder engine, but no further work seems to have been done by Mack on six-wheeled buses until the late 1920s.

Perhaps the most novel developments coming from the fertile minds of Masury and the other Mack engineers at this time,

The experimental Model AD welded sheet metal engine as installed in the prototype AF. After a year of road tests it was decided to shelve the AF truck along with the AD engine.

An artist's rendering of a 1921 Bulldog adapted to use the Christie tracking-laying device, the track of which is shown attached to the underside of the body.

One of four Model ACR rail cars built in 1921, three of which began serving branch lines of a New England railroad early in 1922.

were the new AB and AC Rail Motor Cars. Looking very much like motor buses with railroad-type wheels, headlights, and other auxiliary non-automotive equipment add-ons, the "rail cars" as they were commonly called, added a new dimension to the Mack product line. The first AB rail car, with a vendor supplied body, was finished by the Allentown plant in the fall of 1920. The following year a heavier five-ton model was completed, which was based to some degree on the Bulldog truck. Four of the first Bulldog-type rail cars went into branch line service on two New England railroads during 1921 and 1922.[9]

While the AB rail car could be classed as being based on a highly modified AB truck chassis, such was not the case with the model AC, or "ACR" as it was officially known. Except for the power plant and cooling system, nearly all the other components in the AC rail car were specifically designed to fit the use of this special purpose chassis. The seating capacity of the AC rail car was as high as 50 or 55 passengers, if no express or baggage compartment was desired. The smaller AB rail car had a normal seating capacity of between 21 and 29, or 35 without the baggage area.[10]

The AC rail car frames had to be extra long in order to make a chassis whose overall length was almost 35 feet. The frame side members were originally straight with heavy steel rein-

A 3/4 side view of Bulldog rail car chassis shows use of extra-long straight side rails, reinforced with heavy fish-plates. Note air brakes between wheels of front pony truck.

This rear view of the ACR chassis shows clearly the massive construction of the drive wheels, spring brackets, and brake system.

Allentown plant and New York office officials, with Masury standing on the front truck, pose aboard the ACR rail car during a test run. Plant No. 1, birthplace of the first production AC's in 1916, is in the background.

Direct front view of 1925 ACX rail car built for a Cuban railroad.

forcements, but later units had one-piece frame channels of the "fish-belly" type. The AC rail car also had a special four-speed transmission, with gear ratios proportioned for railroad operating conditions rather than highway service. A huge bevel gear drive rear axle, without a differential, was provided with two optional ratios depending upon potential operating conditions.

Two special railroad drive wheels at the rear, and a four wheel front pony truck, were attached to the frame through springs set in the new rubber shock insulators. A top speed of 41.5 mph in high gear on a level track, and 10.3 mph on a four percent grade could be expected with a rear axle ratio of 3.56 to l., the faster of the optional gearings.[11]

About a dozen of the AC (ACR) rail cars were built up to 1923, with deliveries registered to railroads in Washington, Montana, and North Dakota. The Havana Central Railroad in Cuba took

three of the Bulldog rail cars in 1922 and 1923, being the last purchaser before a new version was introduced. The new ACX rail car had the same Bulldog hood and radiator configuration as the ACR, but was heavier and used a special dual reduction four wheel drive truck at the rear in place of the single drive axle with bevel gear. About ten of the ACX models were built, and most of these in 1925.

In the spring of 1921, the Allentown plant completed a very novel switching locomotive utilizing two Bulldog engines. The new 33 ton locomotive was used mainly to shift railroad cars at plant number 5, the shipping and storage center, and could pull up to 15 cars at one time. It had two Bulldog hoods, one at each end, and a large box-like cab. The switcher also had a straight mechanical drive system that included two drive chains to each axle, and an ingenious transmission arrangement which provided

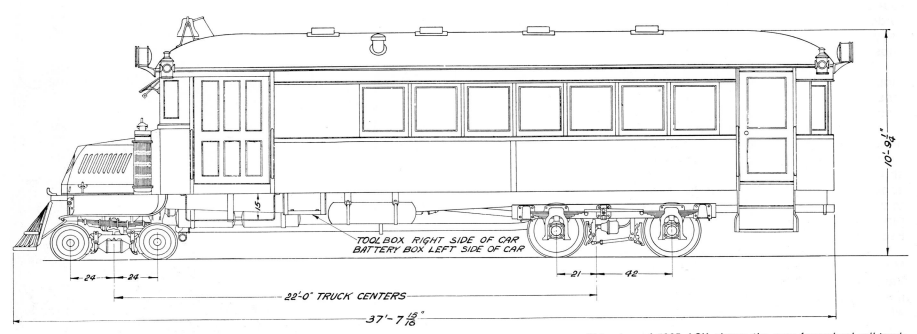

TOOL BOX RIGHT SIDE OF CAR
BATTERY BOX LEFT SIDE OF CAR

22'-0" TRUCK CENTERS

37'-7 15/16"

10'-9 1/4"

Side view of 1925 ACX shows the new four-wheel rail-truck which provided the rail car with an improved riding quality.

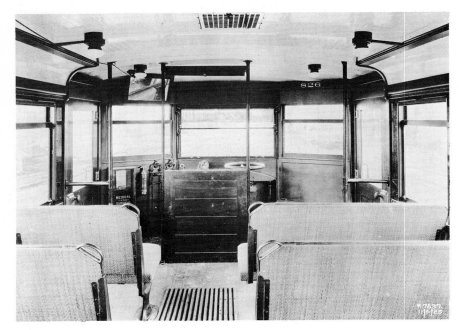

Interior view of the 1925 Model ACX with car body built by the Osgood-Bradley Car Company in Worcester, Massachusetts.

four speeds in either direction.[12] Little product importance was evidently placed on the new "Bulldog Locomotive," as the company concentrated on developing various rail car models until substituting a locomotive building program in 1929.

The development of a system of rubber block inserts for reducing road shocks in a vehicle's chassis parts, was really the most outstanding result of all Mack experimental work taking place during the 1919 and 1920 period. It is believed that the so called "Jump Tests," conducted by the Engineering Department under A. F. Masury, was the starting point in a major effort to reduce the damage caused to chassis parts by excessive road shock and vibration. The tests were basically a highly sophisticated measurement of spring deflection in relationship to the ground impact of pneumatic and solid rubber tires. Masury reported some of the results in an article published during February 1920.[13]

Briefly stated, the test involved the driving of five different Mack trucks up and off a fixed ramp at varying rates of speed. Various calibrated scientific devices were used to accurately measure the deflection of both springs and tires on each truck which sailed off the end of the ramp. Two motion picture

Here the E-15 test truck, with the AD engine, goes off the ramp during the "Jump Tests" of early 1920.

Mack Engineering Department "Jump Tests" were undertaken early in 1920, and recorded by slow-motion movie camera in order to obtain precise data on spring and tire deflections.

cameras, one using a new slow-motion process, recorded each truck as it landed. Masury stated that there was now actual proof that pneumatics reduced road impact by well over 50 percent when compared with the less resilent deflection of solid tires.

The basic problem surrounding the substitution of pneumatic tires for the solid rubber type at this time concerned their extra cost and low mileage life. While pneumatics were soon being ordered by an increasing number of medium-duty Mack AB customers, few AC users wanted the extra cost tires, even if available. At this point Mack engineers started to work out a system of designs for rubber blocks that could be sandwiched between chassis components and frame mounting brackets to absorb some of the vibration caused by road shocks.

The first series of the rubber "cushion connections for vehicle construction," was patented during 1921 and 1922, and given the trade name, "Mack Shock Insulators." New AB bus and truck models were developed during 1921, and introduced in 1922, incorporating the Shock Insulator in the spring brackets and in the steering wheel and gear column mounting. Additional applications for the Shock Insulator principle soon followed, some of which were licensed to other motor vehicle manufacturers.

While these technical advances indicated the serious commitment Mack management placed on developing new vehicle designs, the time honored concept of the relatively slow speed, high torque engine remained a basic Mack vehicle component during the early 1920s. The relative merits of the standard Mack engine, as compared with the characteristics of the relatively high speed competitive power plants coming into vogue at that time, were enunciated by a Mack engineer in a 1921 article entitled, *A Warning from the Air*.[14]

The author of this article, Edwin M. Post, Jr., calling on his experience as a former captain in the United States Air Service and test pilot for the A. E. F., described the basic development of the high compression, high speed, airplane engine during World War I. Post Indicated that the tremendous power of the advanced airplane engines, some as high as 340 hp, was made at a sacrifice of both reliability and length of service life. Also, applying the high speed principles to automobile engines could be understandable since operating costs were not usually a critical factor, owners having a greater interest in their vehicle's hill climbing ability and ultimate power. But in the field of commercial haulage

a truck with such an engine would show its short service life and high maintenance cost, although its initial performance might be outstanding.

The last paragraph of Captain Post's article more or less summed up the future trend of Mack engine design: *In other words, the successful truck of to-day and the future will be one with a slow speed motor with only a moderate mean effective pressure which, if well designed and built, will give its owner not quite the maximum in initial performance, but many years of continued satisfactory service with maintenance and repair expenses cut to a minimum.*

Building A Better Bulldog

In designing and testing new Mack components and vehicles, A. F. Masury and his engineering staff had not overlooked updating the mighty Bulldog. By 1922, it had been about eight years since the basic components of the Bulldog were designed, and six years since the first production models had gone into service.

Masury had evidently been eager to learn of any service problems that should plague the operators of Bulldog or model AB trucks. Starting about 1918, brass plates appeared in all Mack truck cabs with chassis and engine lubrication diagrams. Etched on the plates along with the diagrams was the following statement: *If difficulties occur refer to nearest International Motor Co. Service Station, or to A. F. Masury, Chief Engineer, International Motor Co., 64th St. and West End Ave., New York.*

With a direct pipeline from the ultimate user, Masury must have had a good insight into the strengths and weaknesses of the creations of his Engineering Department.

Up to 1923 there had been no announced changes to the basic design of the Bulldog, the introduction in 1920 of the new 6-1/2 ton and modified five ton models notwithstanding. However, some changes in the engine cooling system had been made during 1917 and 1919, dealing mainly with hood design. An additional change also seems to have been made in radiator design, about 1921, with the use of finned instead of plain tubes. The original radiator tubing was quite small in diameter and the finned ones much larger, thus requiring fewer tubes per radiator section. Since the original semicircular tubing was not soldered into the upper and lower radiator tanks, but held by the expansion

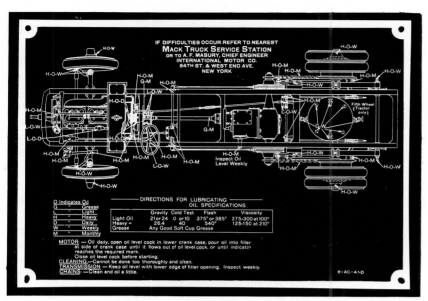

A copy of the chassis lubrication diagram that appeared on a brass plate attached to all Bulldog cab interiors, starting about 1918. Note A. F. Masury's name as an alternate reference in case of difficulties.

A separate brass plate gave precise engine lubrication data, also with Masury's name as a source for satisfaction in case difficulties occurred.

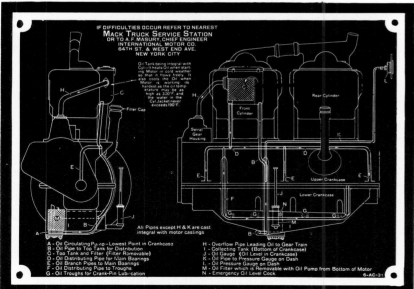

of the tube ends, it is belived that some repair shops had difficulty repairing the tubes when they loosened and began leaking.

Another feature of the original Bulldog was the three-speed transmission. Designed just prior to World War I, it must have been considered more than adequate for its day, but with the experience of World War I military service and increased use by contractors behind it certain shortcomings had evidently been noted. New AC radiator and transmission components were in production by the spring of 1922, and the era of the Bulldog "3-Speeder" was drawing to a close.

The four-speed transmission, with a new low first gear, had improved gear design and other features. While the Bulldog was not meant for high speeds, since it was designed primarily as a solid tired heavy-duty truck, the new transmission provided a greater selection of gear ratios especially needed in construction work. Mack sales literature describing the new transmission speeds characterized them as, "being approximately the same as the three-speed transmission formerly employed." It also stated the first speed to be, "much lower than the second and serving as

As with its three-speed predecessor, the 1922 four-speed transmission was bolted to the differential housing on the jackshaft.

A phantom view of the Type "V" cooling system clearly indicates the flow of air from the Sorrocco blower, mounted behind the clutch housing, to its forced exit through the radiator sections mounted on either side of the Bulldog's cowl.

Section drawing of the flexible rubber steering wheel.

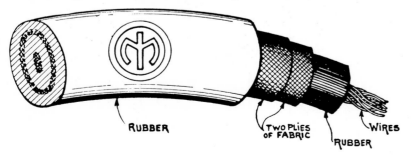

RUBBER TWO PLIES OF FABRIC RUBBER WIRES

an emergency low for use in getting out of excavations, pulling through deep sand and snow and negotiating steep grades."

Another feature of the four-speed transmission was a unique main gear shaft, called the Interrupted Spline Shaft, on which the gears could revolve freely until shifted into engagement on the splined sections of the shaft. This patented construction was claimed to assure perfect alignment of the gears, decreasing noise, aid in shifting, and to generally extend gear life. The original patent on a four-speed Mack transmission was granted in 1917 to A. F. Masury and A. G. Herrreshoff, with Max Frins adding certain refinements in the early 1920s. It is entirely possible that some Bulldog Macks were sold with four-speed transmissions as early as 1921, as Masury felt that actual service in a customer's fleet was the acid test for a new vehicle or component.

The cooling system was greatly improved with the regular production models of the new "4-Speeder" Bulldog Mack. New straight-sided radiator sections with finned tubing replaced the semicircular ones, and a blower, attached directly to the back of the clutch housing, replaced the belt driven fan. The simpler installation of the "Sorrocco" blower in the new Type V (Vee) AC cooling system, proved to be a big improvement. Former Bulldog drivers relate that the fan belt was given to slippage and snapping, due to the fact that the belt was exposed to mud splashed up from the roadway and tended to wear prematurely at times. When the belt broke, the truck was known to surge forward a little due to the sudden release of about ten horsepower, which was needed to drive the fan.

In their effort to make the Bulldog a more efficient truck, the Mack engineers did not overlook refinements in the area of driver comfort. To lessen the vibration transmitted to the driver through the steering gear, especially in a solid tired truck, a new concept of steering wheel design was developed during 1921. The flexible rubber steering wheel used an outer covering of soft rubber over several layers of fabric, rubber, and a core of braided wire. In addition to reducing fatigue by damping chassis vibration, the new steering wheel was considered to have several safety features. It did not become slippery when wet from water or oil, and the rubber rim protected the driver from being hurt on the spoke-ends of the wheel in case of a serious accident.[15] The new wheel became standard equipment on the four-speed Bulldog and AB models during 1922.

During 1921 a completely enclosed Bulldog cab was

developed, called the Year 'Round cab. As with the open and covered cabs, the Year 'Round was of all steel construction. It had sliding doors, with drop windows in them, and a ventilating two-piece windshield. This cab was considered applicable in colder climates, and few Bulldogs were apparently sold with the enclosed cab up to the mid-1920s.

With the effects of the recession of 1921 slowly disappearing during 1922, both the motor truck and construction industries were headed toward boom times—two factors very favorable to the Bulldog Mack. Factory sales of all trucks during 1922 had risen about 80 percent over 1921, and sales in 1923 were almost triple the 1920 figure, for a new record. Business activity in general picked up during this period, with large building projects being particularly favored. Contractors would soon be buying Bulldogs in record numbers, and putting the truck on jobs that even Masury might not have envisioned the AC capable of tackling successfully.

Because of the very nature of their business—bidding on jobs with time limits on the completion of the work—progressive contractors have been usually willing to adopt almost any mechanical or labor saving device to see a project completed on time. Lifting and digging equipment, such as cranes and steam shovels, were found to be very cumbersome when being "walked" from one job to another under their own power. It was finally realized during the 1920s that in addition to serving in dumper service, motor trucks could be utilized in various ways to move heavy equipment, saving much time and effort in the process.

As early as 1920 a truck mounted Universal Crane had made its appearance, and started to prove its facility on small jobs where it did not pay to employ a large machine. Snow removal, ditch digging, pipe laying, and the moving of materials at storage yards became the Universal's forte. The Bulldog chassis with open cab proved to be the most popular mounting platform for such mobile cranes during the mid and late 1920s.

Actually, with the development of the low-bed, "goose-neck," semi-trailer crane work for the Bulldog was child's play when compared to the trucking of heavy steam shovels. By the mid-1920s some contractors were loading their equipment on full trailers, and often used an AC dumper to tow the trailer. However, rapid progress was made during the mid-1920s, by the Rogers Brothers of Albion, Pennsylvania, on a line of heavy-duty

Two new four-speed Bulldogs all decked out in patriotic finery for a local celebration in 1923.

Even heavy transformers could be swung into position with the use of out-riggers for stability.

Use of truck-mounted cranes dates back to the early 1920s. In this 1921 scene, in a Chicago rail yard, a Bulldog-mounted Universal Crane is being used to transfer coal to another Bulldog Mack.

A 1923 four-speed Bulldog and a Bucyrus Model 30-B steam shovel help to widen Queens Boulevard, New York City.

goose-neck trailers especially suited for hauling construction equipment weighing up to 45 tons. Bulldog tractors pulling these trailers and huge shovels or cranes became a common sight by the late 1920s. The 4-Speeder Bulldog tractor, with its extra low first gear, was well adapted to the job of moving gross loads that could easily add up to 50 tons.

A building boom had hit America's big cities by 1924, with taller and taller skyscrapers necessitating deeper and deeper foundations. The 4-Speeder dump truck was now a necessity in the hands of contractors, charged with the digging of an excavation that descended several stories below street level. Because of space restrictions, ramps for the dump trucks tended to be very steep, but the Bulldog Macks could be seen creeping up the grades, some as steep as 33 percent, with several tons of rock and dirt on their backs.[16] However, at some excavations a hoisting engine was used to assist trucks up a steep ramp.

During the mid-1920s Bulldog dump trucks were used to help build New York's Holland Tunnel and Bear Mountain Bridge approaches, and to excavate the site for New York City's huge Columbia-Presbyterian Medical Center complex. Most, if not all, the steel work used in the growing number of large buildings in New York was hauled through heavy mid-town traffic by Bulldog Macks. America's building boom of the 1920s was unprecedented in its extent, and the popularity of the sturdy and versatile Bulldog truck reached new highs by 1925.

The Push for Six Cylinder Power

While the Bulldog Mack had shown its superiority in nearly all lines of heavy service, important changes were taking place in the commercial transport field that would impact on Mack product development in several ways. The popularity of the light-duty "speed truck" during the early 1920s soon led several truck producers to extend the concept to larger medium-duty vehicles. The advent of a growing network of paved highways, improved pneumatic tires for trucks, and the "bus-pneumatic" balloon tire by 1926, helped to foster a market for a large commercial vehicle with a top speed of 50 mph.

The six-cylinder engine was an integral part of the new truck and bus concept, which demanded greater power at more flexible engine speeds. Although large six-cylinder engines had been used on a limited basis in some makes of fire apparatus since

Hauling a 94 foot, 47-ton, girder for the North Branch, New York
highway bridge in the fall of 1924.

just prior to the World War I period, the need for greater power in fire service was most apparent by the mid-1920s. Also, by the end of 1924 there were a dozen makes of buses which offered a six-cylinder model for the growing number of operators wishing to provide faster service for their passengers.[17]

Masury and his engineering staff had been working on several six-cylinder engine concepts since the early 1920s. The rail car program, launched in 1920, had created the need for a very large engine to power a self-propelled unit based on a railroad passenger coach. The AH engine, completed in 1923, had a bore and stroke of 5-1/4 x 7 inches, and was rated at 120 hp. However, the high cost of production, coupled with the low number of units that would be needed, seems to have limited the economic justification of the huge engine. A new rail car named the ACP, using two AC engines, one in each four wheel truck, was developed during 1924.[18]

The AJ engine, which is believed to have been completed in 1924, had a bore and stroke of 4-1/4 x 6 inches and was rated at 100 hp. As stated previously, this engine was most likely used in the Mack Greatcoach, an experimental six wheel bus that was exhibited in the fall of 1924 at the annual convention of the

American Electric Railway Association in Atlantic City. The Greatcoach project was directed by E. R. Gurney,[19] and, no doubt, A. F. Masury had a strong hand in some of the design work. A sloping hood and radiator at the cowl bore the design influences of Masury's pet Bulldog truck. Although no reason has been given for the dropping of the AJ engine project, the long stroke of six inches indicates a relatively slow speed engine, not economically adapted to intercity bus service.

Following closely on the heels of the AJ, was the AL six-cylinder engine and bus project of 1925 and 1926. The new AL engine was produced in two versions before one with a bore and stroke of 4-1/4 x 5 inches was approved for production in 1926. The approved version was rated at 97 hp at 2,200 rpm, indicating that Mack product planners had finally decided on a relatively high speed engine to power the new intercity AL bus. Power and speed were very important to the success of the new Mack bus, since it had been designed for intercity and suburban service where the runs were longer and more grades were likely to be encountered than on local city routes.

As with the Greatcoach before it, the AL bus had the earmarks of the Bulldog's design influences. Its slanting and tapered frontal appearance aped the Bulldog's hood design, but unlike the AC the AL's radiator was located at an angle in the front, and not at the cowl. The use of Bulldog inspired sheet

Some of the New York Engineering staff and other Mack personnel turned out for the test run of the Mack Greatcoach, with six-cylinder AJ engine. Chief Engineer Masury is seated behind the wheel in this photo taken in the fall of 1924.

The Model AL six-cylinder bus, introduced in 1926, was found to be highly adaptable to some businesses needing a relatively high-speed truck in the medium capacity range.

metal work where it was not functionally useful, showed Masury's strong influence over product design.

An article in a contemporary trade publication announcing the new AL six-cylinder bus, contained the following pregnant statement: "Probably few laymen can appreciate the endless amount of work entailed in the construction of a new model and the intricacy of the problem faced by the engineers."[20] This was the understatement of the year, for at least three different engines and six chassis had been engineered and constructed before satisfactory designs were approved.

A former engineer, who worked on the AL bus project in 1925, is a witness to the long hours and the strong determination shown by Chief Engineer Masury. Henry Miller, retired Mack executive engineer, remembered that starting on New Year's Day the two men worked closely and continuously on the designs, putting in numerous seven-day weeks without a break. Finally, on one Saturday in the spring, Miller announced that he would not be in the next day, as it was Easter and he was taking his mother to church. Masury was, at first, somewhat perturbed, but later in the day approached Miller again and informed him that he too would not be in the next day, as he was also going to take his mother to church.[21]

The new low-slung AL bus chassis had a natural appeal to the moving and storage operator needing a speed truck in the medium-duty range of about three tons capacity. Within a year AL "bus commercials" were being sold in small numbers to a growing segment of the trucking industry, in which the economics of faster, although higher cost delivery, and relatively high value freight, could be matched.

The AL engine was quickly adapted for fire service, as the largest Mack fire engines being offered at that time had a pumping capacity of about 600 gallons per minute. A triple combination pumper was completed in the spring of 1926, having the AL engine hidden under a longer than normal Bulldog hood. Model AC hoods, starting with the Type V cooling system, had 10 louvers on each side, but the new AL pumper had 13 louvers.

First Bulldog fire engine having the Model AL six-cylinder engine. This unit was delivered to Phillipsburg, New Jersey, in the spring of 1926.

The Mack AP engine set up with special clutch and winch assembly for cable tool drilling and for pulling well casing in the oil fields.

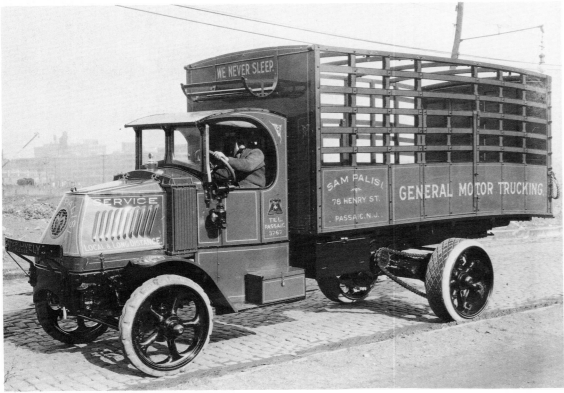

A typical 1924 3-1/2 ton capacity Bulldog with Mack-built rack body for use in general haulage service.

With the use of the model AL engine in the traditional Model AC chassis, a problem arose in vehicle model designations. At first, the Bulldog fire apparatus having AL engines were referred to as AL's, but a system of numbered fire apparatus "types," or models, was also adopted to avoid confusion. For the most part, the "types" were based on the fire apparatus equipment placed on the chassis, rather than the commercial model of the truck serving as the running gear for the fire engine.

An even larger six-cylinder Mack engine, designated the AP, was developed by 1926. The new AP was similar to the AC engine, having a bore and stroke of 5 x 6 inches. As a power plant for oil field cable-drilling work, sales literature later described the AP engine as, "A modern engine developing 150 hp with a speed range of from 200 to 2,000 revolutions per minute." Also, that, "..final design may be credited to the cooperation of the best-known men in the oil fields of Texas, Oklahoma, Colorado, Wyoming and Montana."[22] While the AP was evidently developed as a portable power plant, it would soon be adapted to fire service, and later to the highway haulage and heavy construction fields as a Super-duty Bulldog truck.

The Bulldog in High Gear

The boom period of the mid-1920s saw the Bulldog Mack reach a degree of public recognition unequalled by any other make of truck, and only surpassed, perhaps, by the Model T Ford and Rolls-Royce automobiles. Capitalizing on this public awareness were the artists, cartoonists, and general illustrators, who used the general form of the Bulldog Mack to typify the brute power and massiveness of a heavy-duty truck. Bulldog trucks also found their way into the lives of the younger generation by a most direct route.

By 1926 toy makers were having a field day producing Bulldog trucks in almost every possible scale. The toy trucks ranged in size from the tiny pot metal Tootsietoy, for pushing around the living room floor, to the largest pressed-steel pedal-car, for the more athletic youngster. At this time some of the most famous and enduring of the Bulldog toys were those made of cast iron by Arcade and Hubley. The Mack Advertising Department was not oblivious to the subtle promotional value connected with the miniatures, and briefly offered a special sales folder showing selected toys available from the company. The

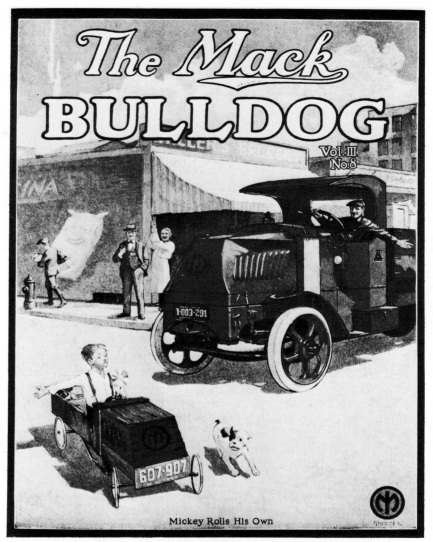

The house organ, The Mack Bulldog, *made its appearance in 1920. Mickey became a regular cover feature in 1923. These magazines are collectors' items today.*

sales folder was entitled, *Practical Toys for Future Mack Transport Men.*[23]

A really outstanding house organ called *The Mack Bulldog* was started by the Advertising Department early in 1920. *The Mack Bulldog* appeared as a monthly at first, but following the recession of the early 1920s, it was suspended for a few months during late 1922 and early 1923. Full color covers were standard by May 1922, and a young boy named Mickey became a regular cover feature during 1923. For several years the covers traced the exploits of Mickey and his girl friend Mary, which somehow involved a Bulldog truck or other Mack commercial vehicle. Aside from the cover humor, *The Mack Bulldog* contained interesting articles on component improvements, new vehicles, and unique hauling operations involving, of course, the Mack nameplate.

The Mack Advertising Department also produced numerous editions of catalogs on the Bulldog truck, which were richly illustrated with half-tones showing all the components in great detail. For those desiring lots of truck photos, there was the trade booklet series, started in 1920, which covered every major industry from bottling to lumbering by 1926. Mack advertising was based mainly on a direct appeal to certain specific industries at this time, rather than by ads placed in popular periodicals.

There was strong competition from several other prominent truck manufacturers during the early 1920s, and it is interesting to note their specific strong points in relation to the Bulldog truck by 1926. The most well-known of these, and perhaps Mack's arch rival at this point, was the White truck. Starting in 1919, White had abandond chain-drive in its heavy-duty models, substituting a unique form of double reduction. A conventional single reduction bevel gear rear axle was used in conjunction with cast steel wheels, each having an enlarged hub containing an internal gear which provided the second reduction. As a sales pitch, the White double reduction was sometimes likened to an enclosed chain-drive, since the internal gear drove the wheel at a distance of several inches from the center of the hub, providing a leverage effect similar to that which was claimed for the rear wheel sprocket on a chain-drive Mack. Some contractors liked the double reduction Whites, but they were more often found in the building supply or general hauling fields.

Garford and Kelly-Springfield were two well-made chain-drive trucks from the World War I era, which gradually switched to other drive systems and declined in popularity during the

Competition between Mack and White grew more apparent by the mid-1920s with the gradual demise of smaller truck builders. Note lower chassis height of the heavy-duty White on the left.

A mid-1920s seven-ton Kelly-Springfield with hood design reminiscent of the Bulldog's. The Kelly truck disappeared about 1927.

Kelly-Springfield Truck, Model KS 70—7 Tons

1920s. The Kelly had used a Renault-type hood and radiator at the cowl, but started building some conventional looking trucks by 1924. However, the five and seven-ton capacity Kelly trucks were still being built in 1926 with chain-drive and a hood and radiator configuration not too unlike the Bulldog Mack. The Kelly ceased production in 1927, and the Garford was produced up to the early 1930s.

Packard and Pierce-Arrow trucks had also established quality reputations by World War I, and each had supplied several thousand military trucks to the Allied armies. Both trucks had used worm-drive for many years and, except during the height of World War I, their production had been more of an adjunct of the basic automobile businesses of their respective companies. This situation became manifest during the recession of 1921, when demand for heavy-duty trucks tumbled sharply. With the introduction of a new automobile model in 1923, Packard quietly withdrew from the truck building field. Like White, Packard had made an attempt to sell to firms in the contracting business, but had made better penetration of the building supply and general haulage fields. However, unlike Packard, White had discontinued its line of passenger cars to concentrate on trucks by 1920.

The Pierce-Arrow truck, on the other hand, was continued in spite of rumors that it would be dropped and the company make only pleasure cars.[24] Engines in Pierce-Arrow trucks used four valves for each cylinder, instead of the normal two; and two spark plugs per cylinder, instead of one. Better fuel economy, due to better ignition and scavenging of exhaust gases, was claimed with the larger combined valve areas in the Dual Valved Pierce engine. However, a brake horsepower of only 63 was stated for this engine, versus the 74 brake horsepower of the AC engine, which had a slightly larger bore but a shorter stroke. Pierce-Arrow trucks were found mostly in general hauling, but were also used heavily in the building supply field and by some contractors.

By the middle of the 1920s, the Mack model line was the most complete of all manufacturers of quality commercial vehicles. The basic strategy of the product planners at this point seems to have been a move to truck equipment, so that Mack sales outlets could offer complete, ready to use, vehicles. In theory it was a good idea, as access to truck chassis data would be a simple matter to those Mack engineers also designing dump bodies, hoists, and winches. The result would be truck equipment that fitted Mack commercial vehicles exactly, and gave Mack salesmen the chance to make a convenient package deal for a customer.

Truck bodies of various kinds had been built at both Allentown and New York City plants since the days prior to World War I. With the great demand for Bulldog trucks in the contracting field, dump bodies of from four to ten yards capacity had become almost a specialty item for the Allentown plant by 1925. A steel body with a renewable floor, which could stand the pounding of heavy rocks longer than previous designs, was followed into production during 1926 by the Mack Screw Hoist. The new underbody lifting device was the mechanical equivalent of the popular Heil under-body hydraulic hoist, and soon Bulldog dump trucks were being sold with completely Mack-built body and hoist equipment.

Mack Underbody Screw Hoist showing twin-screw mechanism fully extended and dump body raised to full tilt.

Collapsible boots fitted over the screws to protect their precision mechanism from harmful grit.

The Mack Aluminum Container and Ramp Track was a noble experiment to improve the method of handling less-than-carload freight shipments. Photo taken in 1926.

The most interesting body concept to come from the Mack engineers' drawing boards at this time, was the Aluminum Container for less-than-carload freight. The new container units were first used in conjunction with a large eastern railroad, and were hauled to and from the freight yards by Bulldog Macks during 1925. There was also a Mack "ramp track" for unloading the containers at the consignee's location, which provided a complete system for handling the labor saving units.

A line of Mack built winches was also readied, by 1926, for use with model AB and AC trucks. The winches were driven from the standard Mack truck transmissions, either through a side-mounted power take-off, or an extension countershaft on the AC. The winches had extended winch heads to clear the sides of the standard AB and AC cabs for pulling from the front with manila rope.

Various refinements were made in the Bulldog truck during the mid-1920s. Radiator shutters were developed about 1924, but did not become popular until 1925 or 1926. The shutters helped to control heat loss from the cooling system on cold days, so as to keep the engine at the recommended operating temperature of 180 degrees. The vertical shutters were controlled manually from the cab. Later, a thermostat was incorporated in a by-pass, which restricted the flow of cold water in the engine but opened automatically as the engine warmed up to allow a normal flow of heated water to be cooled by the radiator.

During 1925 a prototype of an improved four-cylinder AC engine was completed. The concept of the removable engine head stemmed from the World War I era, and was a feature which gave mechanics better access to valves and combustion chambers for servicing. All Mack power plants designed during the 1920s had removable heads about twice as thick as heads on competitive engines, and the twin heads on the new AC engine were no execption. Evidently, it was several years before the new AC "High Hat" engine was phased into production, as Bulldog sales literature printed as late as 1927 still illustrated the AC

Close-up of four-speed Bulldog hood gives good view of manually controlled radiator shutters.

engine with non-removable heads. However, by 1925 air cleaners were available on all Mack commercial vehicles, and other improvements were being tested for introduction at a later date.

An improved tractor version of the AC, with smaller diameter wheels and special curved rear spring horns, was introduced in 1925. This special rear end frame arrangement was also used on the 156 inch wheel base Bulldog dump truck, due to its heavier construction features. Bulldog tractors for pulling semi-trailers were still built in the basic 7, 10, 13, and 15 ton trailer-load capacities at this time.

The original Mack Universal, "Waffle Iron," fifth wheel was discontinued by 1924, due to the popularity of more efficient trailer coupling devices. However, Mack trailers in both two and four wheel versions, built since the early 1920s in limited quantities, were increasing in popularity. The Mack trailers were built from some AB and AC truck components, and apparently offered only on a custom basis, as they were not advertised.

The motor truck industry prospered for the most part during the growth period of the 1920s, recording a quadrupling of total trucks sold between the recession year of 1921 and the boom year of 1926. Factory sales of all trucks sold in 1921 were 148,052, having dropped back to almost the 1917 level, but shot up to a new record of 608,617 units in 1926.[25]

As a natural consequence of the spreading reputation of the Mack product line and good business conditions, Mack sales and profits reached new highs during 1925 and 1926. Between 1920 and 1926 Mack sales had doubled, being $34 million in the former, and $69 million in the latter. Net profit had more than tripled during this period, reaching $8.9 million in 1926, up from $2.6 million recorded in 1920.[26] It had been decided to adopt the name Mack Trucks, Inc., during 1922, for the name of the holding company, and the title International Motor Truck Corporation was dropped at this time. However, the International Motor Company remained as the main operating unit of Mack Trucks, and continued to appear on the name plates as the builder of all Bulldog trucks and other Mack products during the 1920s.

Wisely, Mack management had followed an expansionist policy following the World War I period, with new facilities being

The 1925 tractor version of the Bulldog with curved rear spring horns and smaller diameter wheels to reduce overall height.

Elevated view of the basic AC chassis shows the straight frame construction.

added on almost a regular basis all through the 1920s. The first and most important facility acquired was the plant of the Wright-Martin Aircraft Corporation in New Brunswick, New Jersey, which could produce iron, bronze, and aluminum castings in both quality and quantity. The New Brunswick plant had built several thousand high performance Hispano-Suiza aircraft engines for the Allied military cause, and had also made the renowned Simplex automobile prior to 1918. During 1920 the new plant was earmarked to become the source for all Mack geared com-

ponents, which eventually included transmissions, jackshafts, steering gears, and differential carriers. Additions were made to both the Allentown and Plainfield factories as needed, with the large assembly plant, Number 5-C, being completed at Allentown by 1926.

A large multi-story plant was erected during 1925 in Long Island City, as a combined service station and body building facility for the New York City area. This building was part of a multi-million dollar program to expand and upgrade the Mack branch system throughout the United States and Canada. It is interesting to note that the new Long Island City plant became the

Basic AC chassis without radiator and sheet metal shows relatively simple, but rugged construction.

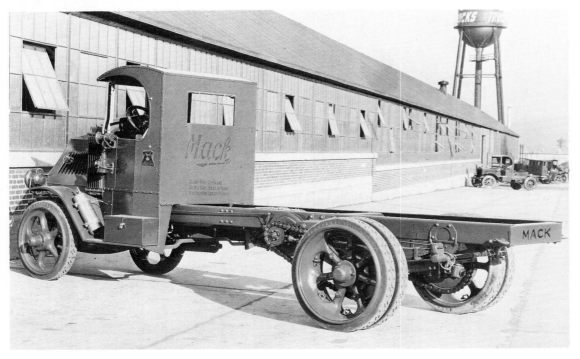

A left-hand side view of the AC Bulldog shows the Prest-O-Lite gas tank for the acetylene headlights, attached to the front fender. The side lights and tail light used kerosene oil, in most cases.

headquarters of A. F. Masury and his engineering staff, which were transferred from the old 64th Street building along with the experimental work. By 1926 the 64th Street building was relegated mainly to routine local sales and service work, and for use as a storage garage. A new executive office had been leased in the Cunard Building at 25 Broadway in New York City, during 1921, and most of the major departments transferred there from the former headquarters building on 64th Street.

The Mack organization had achieved a modern and progressive image by 1926, despite the fact that an important part of Mack production consisted of trucks having chain-drive, a product feature that was generally considered passe by 1920. While important advances were made in designing several efficient six-cylinder engines to keep pace with the trends in the industry during the mid-1920s, basic design philosophy remained of a conservative nature. The Code of the Mack Safety League, started in 1925, gave an indication that Mack commercial vehicles would not be designed with speed as one of their main features. A driver, who joined the League, signed a statement that included the following last lines:[27]

I will always drive with
—F I R S T—
Care, Comfort, and Courtesy.
—L A S T—
Speed.

Flexibility of the heat-treated Bulldog frame is quite apparent in this late 1925 view. Note punched out M A C K in rear cross member, which design was used for about one year, disappearing in 1926.

Building AC engines in special revolving frames at the Plainfield Plant in 1924.

Truck Trends of the Late Twenties

What had started with a sigh and the sloganed concept of a "return to normalcy," in 1920, had become an almost defiant roar with much of the American public feeling there was "no place to go but up," by 1929. In retrospect, the Roaring Twenties was an era that spawned, with few pauses, a continuous growth of the general business tempo, a great degree of social ferment, and an individual mobility that had previously been unknown to the American life style.

Helping to tie together America's "manifest destiny of the twenties," were the thousands of miles of new highways, many impressive new bridges and tunnels, as well as a record auto and truck production which reached combined sales of slightly over 5.3 million units during 1929.[1] There is no denying that speed and daring played an important part in the mass psychology of the 1920s, with such men as the auto racer and World War I flying ace, Eddie Rickenbacher, and the transatlantic aviator, Charles Lindbergh, being acclaimed as national heros.

The importance of speed as an influence in automobile construction was quite marked during the 1920s, with the more exclusive makes leading the way in longer, lower, and more powerful designs. The moderate priced cars usually followed the trends set by the leaders, with most new concepts having a "ripple effect" throughout the automotive industry. It was quite obvious, by the late 1920s, that truck producers were following in the footsteps of the automobile builders, with most of the light and medium-duty truck models introduced after 1926 tending to resemble passenger cars. The relative success of the low-slung, six-cylinder bus chassis in the meduim-duty truck field also had a strong influence at this time. The use of relatively high-speed six-cylinder engines, four wheel brakes, balloon tires, and comfortable coupe-type cabs, became the rule rather than the exception in most new truck models by 1927.

A wild west show, based in Oklahoma, used its mid-1920s Bulldogs for hauling baggage, pulling wagons to and from the lot, and in street parades.

The typical new truck chassis was lower in overall frame height, resulting in a vehicle that was less likely to overturn in an accident due to its lower center of gravity. Even headlights, sheet metal and dash-board instrument panels followed passenger car design. Such improvements eventually found their way into the larger, heavy-duty models, whose designs tended to be more fixed than the lighter series. To sum up, while the new six-cylinder trucks were much faster than the four-cylinder models of the same tonnage rating, they were really much safer too, due mainly to the quicker stopping ability of their four wheel brakes, and better skid control afforded by the improved tread design on their balloon tires.

Mack engineering had stressed the importance of strength and simplicity in all Mack products from the earliest days. The continued use of chain-drive as a fixed and optional component in the AC and AB truck models, respectively, is an example of this policy. The traditional four-cylinder Mack power plants were almost indestructable, under even some of the most strenuous circumstances, due in great measure to the special heat treatment for the toughness of their critical parts. Also, as stressed in various articles and product sales literature, Mack engines developed their maximum power at relatively slow crankshaft speeds, which was considered an important factor in prolonging the useful life of any internal combustion engine.

As late as September 1924, Chief Engineer Masury had indicated he favored four-cylinder engines for motor bus service, even though six-cylinder power plants for buses were coming into vogue.[2] It is highly unlikely at that time for Masury to have considered six-cylinder engines any more favorably for the relatively slower speed AB and AC trucks, as regular six-cylinder Mack truck models were not introduced until 1928 and 1929, about four years later. However, it must be understood that many fleet operators, especially those serving large urban areas, favored the general economy and long service life of the four-cylinder Mack engines. Also, Masury was well aware of what the big fleet managers were considering important in truck design, as he maintained an important role in both sales and service operations for Mack all through the 1920s. Even though there was much in Masury's conservative engineering policy that was commendable, the trends in truck design and truck use would have a strong influence on Mack truck models introduced in the late 1920s.

State motor vehicle laws had an increasing influence on truck design during the late 1920s, with gross vehicle weight sections creating the most pressure for change. At this time many states recognized the desirability of spreading a heavy vehicle load over six instead of four wheels, with some states allowing up to 12,000 pounds additional gross weight for the third axle. By 1928 Illinois regulations allowed four-wheeled trucks a maximum 24,000 pounds g. v. w., but six-wheelers could range up to 40,000 pounds g. v. w., for an additional eight tons of truck and cargo.[3]

With the legalization of the much higher gross vehicle weight for six-wheelers, many truckers in such states as California, Illinois, Missouri, and Pennsylvania took a great interest in their development. Some heavy haulers converted their heavy-duty four-wheeled trucks to six-wheelers by the use of an attachment axle, usually being located behind the truck's rear drive axle. Utility six wheel units, made in California, were very popular as conversion axles by 1929, and many Bulldog Macks were made into six-wheelers in midwest and western states about this time.

Along with the liberalization of the gross vehicle weight laws, some states allowed an additional trailer to be attached behind the usual tractor and semi-trailer combination. By 1928 some states allowed gross vehicle combinations weighing up to 50,000 or 60,000 pounds.[4] By the early 1930s, Illinios had a 72,000 pound limit on a tractor and two-trailer combination, but no restrictions on the number of four-wheeled trailers that could be tagged on behind the power unit.[5] Of course, the amount of power and traction suppplied by the truck or truck-tractor pulling the trailer-train, were the practical limitations governing the weight of such combinations.

Bulldog tank trucks were used by some midwestern petroleum companies to pull as many as two four-wheeled tank trailers by the late 1920s. On the West Coast, Bulldog tankers with third axle attachments were also used extensively in the petroleum industry, some in combination with six-wheeled tank trailers. It must be remembered that such Samson-like feats of strength were performed by Bulldog trucks having the standard AC four-cylinder engine and four-speed transmission. The fact that standard AC trucks were rebuilt to increase their carrying capacity by upwards of 50 percent and could also pull loads equal to, or even double, their own gross weight, certainly is a tribute to the basic engineering philosophy of Hewitt, Masury, and the

Six wheelers became popular in many western states in order to meet legal restrictions on axle loadings. This mid-1920s 4-Speeder was used to haul a tremendous payload of gasoline in Southern California.

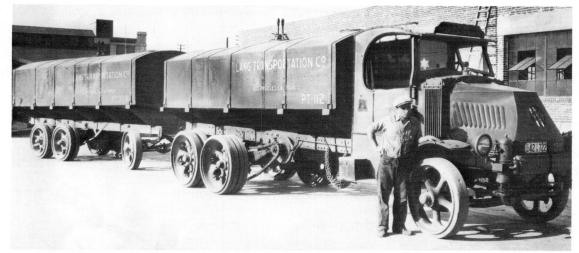

An attachment axle has just been fitted to this Chicago-based petroleum tanker. Note special cab on this Bulldog that was preferred in some cities for use with gasoline delivery trucks.

A rebuilt Bulldog with balloon tires serving a Midwestern oil company in 1931. Such a truck and trailer combination must have weighed about 100,000 pounds with payload, but the low-speed high-torque AC engine had the power to move it right along.

other Mack engineers responsible for making the Bulldog truck a "living legend."

By the late 1920s some states recognized the advantage of pneumatic tires over solids in reducing damage to roads by heavily laden trucks, and these states allowed as much as a two or three ton higher gross vehicle weight for those trucks using pneumatics. The liberalization of some state gross vehicle weight laws in regard to the use of pneumatics, really coincided with the perfection of the low-pressure "bus-balloon" tire about 1926. Up to this time the larger pneumatic truck tires had been of the high-pressure type, and were not only very expensive but usually had only a fraction of the life span of a solid tire of the same load capacity. However, by 1928 great interest in balloon tires was being shown by owners of heavier trucks, and several Bulldog Macks were produced that year with balloon tires as original equipment.

Another consequence of the state motor vehicle weight laws was the adoption of gross vehicle weight ratings by truck manufacturers in place of the usual rating of truck models by their carrying capacity. Under the new "straight rating" system the gross vehicle weight was used as part of the model description, and the model's g. v. w. was then broken down by its basic chassis weight, the body allowance, and load capacity. This system made it much easier for both the manufacturer and user to conform to the local state laws, which were the ultimate governing factor in the use of heavy-duty trucks.

With the Bulldog truck hanging onto the contracting field as though it was a private domain and even making a better penetration of the building supply field, the future of the Mack AC looked good in 1927, despite a sizable drop in production due to a recession in the truck industry that year. During 1928 a dump trailer, operating with a power take-off equipped AC tractor, became popular with building supply firms in some cities, since the unit greatly increased the payload a single driver could deliver to a construction site in one trip. The tractor-dump trailer units were all solid tired, as were nearly all other Bulldog trucks built up to 1928.

While some of the trends in the late 1920s, such as increased use of high speed six-cylinder engines, faster vehicle speeds, pneumatic tires, and more elaborate cabs, seemed to have been out pacing the Bulldog truck, competition was still learning a trick or two from this mighty Mack. Renewed interest in chain-drive was shown by some other truck manufacturers during 1927 and 1928. The International Harvester Company, which never had any corporate connection with the International Motor Company, introduced several chain-drive dump truck models at

Increased payloads could be handled by this Bulldog tractor and Warner dump-trailer combination. Note twin-piston Wood hydraulic hoist mounted on trailer.

A close-up of power take-off on top of AC transmission used to actuate hydraulic pump on dump trailer.

this time. Also, the Sterling Motor Truck Company increased its line of chain-drive trucks to include 11 such models by 1929. The increased use of chain-drive by two truck builders, who had either dropped or used this feature only on their largest models since the World War I period, was certainly a vindication of the faith that Masury had shown in the chain-drive Bulldog since its first testing in 1925.

Even the Bulldog's pugnacious look and resolute lines were aped by two other truck builders. Besides the heavy-duty Kelly truck, mentioned in Chapter II, another obvious copy of the Bulldog was the Model 41 Indiana, introduced early in 1925.[6] The new heavy-duty, worm-drive Indiana was christened the "Big

Steve" by its builders, the Indiana Truck Corporation. The front bumper, hood, general cab design, and sheet metal skirting, were all very similar to the Mack AC. However, the slanting hood covered the frontal placement of the radiator, and it had horizontal instead of vertical louvers. The Big Steve was built up to 1927 and was rated variously as a 4-5 or 5-7 ton capacity unit.

The most formidable competition ever faced by the four-speed Bulldog came from the Sterling Motor Truck Company of Milwaukee, Wisconsin, whose line of four and six-cylinder, chain-drive dump trucks had gained good acceptance by the late 1920s. While the Sterling was, to some degree, an assembled truck, using Waukesha engines for the most part, it did have some unique engineering features and always maintained a favorable reputation among heavy haulers. Nearly all models came equipped with a wood-lined frame, which was supposed to absorb some of the destructive road shocks transmitted to the chassis and its components by the wheels and springs. Since the wood was compressible, it was impossible to employ rivets to permanently secure the components tightly to the frame, and so Sterling was one of the few trucks to always use a bolted chassis construction. The use of bolted construction has been highly touted in the truck industry since the 1960s, as a means for the quick replacement of damaged chassis components.

The Sterling DC series, rated at 4-1/2 to 8-1/2 tons capacity, offered pneumatic tires as optional equipment, and contractors started buying such balloon-tired dump trucks with the idea of speeding up their excavating jobs. A standard four-speed transmission could be supplemented with a three-speed auxiliary transmission, providing 12 forward and three reverse speeds. The use of the higher-speed six-cylinder engines and optional auxiliary transmissions provided a great flexibility in both power and speed.

The largest Sterlings, the EC series with top capacities of 10 or 11 tons, had six-speed transmissions with constant-mesh gears as standard equipment, and four or six-cylinder engines for a top horsepower of 98. In comparison, the largest Bulldog was officially rated at 7-1/2 tons capacity, although it was common knowledge among heavy haulers that the AC chassis could easily handle an almost 100 percent overload, and often did! And while six-cylinder engines were not available in the Bulldog until 1931, the AC engine was rated a a maximum of 76 horsepower at 1,800 rpm, by 1930.

The Indiana Big Steve model had hood and bumper configuration similar to the Bulldog Mack, and was rated as a heavy-duty truck.

Chain-drive Sterling six-cylinder trucks became a major competitor of the Mack AC during the late 1920s. A Model EC29-66KU Sterling, rated at 29,000 g. v. w., serving a building supply firm.

Another standard Sterling feature was a large coupe-type cab with large hinged doors, although some contractors preferred the simpler covered cab which was similar to the Bulldog's standard cab. Other points of difference included the location and application of service and parking brakes, angle of inclination of the steering gear assembly, and cooling system design.

In short, the Roaring Twenties seems to have fostered a technology whose ideal was power and speed, with even the design of heavy-duty trucks being effected by this constant striving. Masury and his engineering staff had been working on many new vehicle designs during the 1925 to 1927 period, and the Bulldog had not been overlooked in their plan for a superior Mack product line.

A New Product Mix

In the fall of 1927 Mack announced the introduction of the Model AK truck of 3-1/2 to 5-tons capacity. The AK was described

as being the answer for those operators needing a faster truck of moderate capacity, that was also capable of better road performance than heavier models. Sales literature also indicated that, "...weight restrictions of increasing severity in several important states..." had led operators "...to seek other means of achieving high ton-mileage than the simple expedient of carrying heavy loads."[7]

The AK was, in some ways, a dual reduction version of the lightest capacity Model AC, with certain important changes in keeping with the trend in truck design. New features included the following: four wheel brakes with vacuum booster, sharper turning radius than the standard AC, and a four-speed transmission, mounted in Shock Insulator equipped support brackets, had an optional high speed reverse gear. Rubber Shock Insulators were also used in cab supports and spring brackets, and the dual reduction axle was of larger dimension than that used in the smaller AB models. However, a chain-drive version of the AK was also available which required certain modifications to the rear spring and brake designs.

The Model AK Mack was introduced in the fall of 1927. Note four-wheel brakes, six-spoked wheels, shock insulator spring brackets, and external gasoline filler spout and tank gauge.

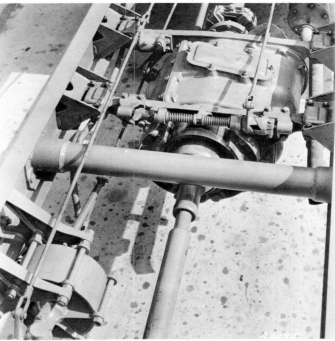

A close-up of the new dual reduction AK rear axle. Note the vacuum booster brake cylinder mounted between frame side rail and drive shaft.

The AK also had it own four-speed transmission mounted in rubber shock insulators. Note also torque insulator on drive shaft just ahead of transmission, and parking brake just behind.

The AK engine was of the monoblock design, having its four cylinders cast integrally, but with pair-cast detachable aluminum heads. Pistons were also made of aluminum and the connecting rods were of a tubular construction. The bore and stroke was 4-5/8 x 6 inches, only slightly smaller than the 5 x 6 dimensions of the AC engine. The slight difference in the bore indicates that the same basic block could have been used for both AC and AK engines, and by 1929 the improved monoblock AC engine, introduced in 1928, was substituted in AK four-cylinder models.

While the hood, radiator, and cab looked almost exactly like the famous AC Mack, there were subtle differences in addition to the afore-mentioned major ones, and the Model AK should never really be called a "Bulldog." The AK had an enlarged version of the covered steel cab used on the AC, and a wooden-framed two-piece windshield, set at a slight angle, was available. While the

gasoline tank was located under the drivers's seat, it had the filler spout and a tank gauge on the outside, so the seat cushion did not have to be moved in order to fill the tank, as in the Model AC. Also the AK had cast steel wheels of six spokes each, front and rear, while the AC's steel wheels had five spokes in front and seven in the rear.

While the first AK units were equipped with solid tires, during 1928 many were sold with the improved balloon type pneumatic which were usually mounted on Budd steel disc wheels. The use of balloon tires certainly added to the AK's performance, with the added speed now possible being adequately controllable by its vacuum assisted four wheel braking system. While some traditional users of chain-drive Macks purchased the AK with this type of drive, AK dual reduction output was always much greater than the production of the chain-drive version. Even

The AK four-cylinder engine was rated at about 70 horsepower, but was discontinued by the end of 1928 with the substitution of a new AC engine.

When the AK was first introduced, solid tires were standard, but by 1929 nearly all units came equipped with balloon tires.

A 1928 AK belonging to a New York area moving and storage company. Balloon tires gave this unit a respectable road speed, and a company driver stated that it drove "like a limousine" as compared to the firm's solid-tired ACs.

The AK street flusher served a dual purpose as can be noted from plowing equipment mounted on the front. Note city's name in French on the right side.

The flushing equipment was mounted on a 1928 AK chassis by Bickle Fire Engines, Ltd., Woodstock, Ontario, Canada. The name is in English on the left side, indicating the bilingualism of Quebec Province.

many customers in the construction and building supply fields purchased AK's with dual reduction.

By 1929 the AK four-cylinder truck had proved itself as a speedy commercial vehicle of heavy-duty construction that was capable of handling a wide variety of hauling duties. Some had been sold to petroleum companies and used as tank trucks, and others were used in the construction and building supply industries as dumpers or with concrete mixer bodies. Most AK's were used in large urban areas to haul the daily needs of the inhabitants, from food to fuel. A few long wheel-based AK Macks, with balloon tires, were even used in the moving industry where their speed and hauling capabilities found utility.

The really outstanding Mack product achievement of 1927 was the introduction of a new series of fire apparatus having the AP six-cylinder, 150 horsepower engine, and pump capacities of 750 to 1,000 gallons per minute. The new "AP" fire engine, like the AK truck, had four wheel brakes with a vacuum booster for faster and more powerful braking ability. Balloon tires, electric starting and lighting, and dual reduction were standard features. Chain-drive was available as an option.

With the most powerful Mack engine under its Bulldog-like hood, four-speed transmission, balloon tires, and power brakes to help ease it through traffic, the "AP" fire engine had the impor-

tant capabilities that were being required by many urban fire departments in the late 1920s. The basic AP pumper was later called the Type 15, following a new system of designating Mack fire apparatus models based on the nature of their power and fire fighting equipment, rather than by the engine or chassis model used in their construction.

In the fall of 1927, a huge Type 15 chain-drive pumper was delivered to the City of Seattle, Washington. However, before delivery the Type 15 stopped at Berkeley, California, where a Byron-Jackson 1,000 g. p. m., series-parallel, multi-stage centrifugal pump was installed by its manufacturer. As an indication of the Type 15's power and capacity, it pumped at a rate of 1,973 g. p. m. during acceptance tests, or almost double the rated capacity.[8] In the summer of 1927 two of the new dual reduction Type 15 pumpers were delivered to the City of San Francisco, but these were apparently equipped with Hale rotary gear pumps of a lesser capacity.

Mack engineers developed an engine-driven mechanical hoist for aerial ladders in conjunction with a special AP powered tractor, with the first unit being delivered to Kearny, New Jersey, in 1928. The Mack experimental shop at 64th Street had developed a spring powered aerial ladder in the early twenties, but the new device was a big advance and completely

One of two Type 15 pumpers with Model AP engines, and dual reduction drives, delivered to the City of San Francisco in 1927.

This AP aerial ladder had the first Mack-built engine driven hoisting units, and was delivered to Kearney, New Jersey, in the fall of 1928.

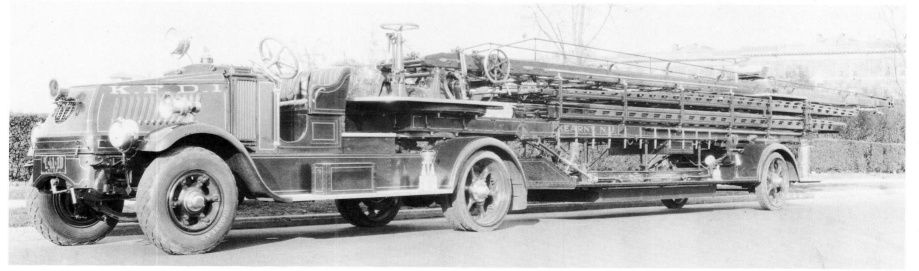

superseded the earlier type. The new aerial ladder came in 65, 75 and 85 foot lengths, and used a power take-off from the transmission on the tractor to drive a vertical shaft which passed directly through the center line of both the fifth wheel and ladder turntable.

During 1928 the AL bus chassis was adapted for fire apparatus use and achieved a moderate degree of success in this new role. The earlier AB bus chassis had already shown the desirability of using the low-slung "bus-commercial" in fire apparatus service, with the first such units going to Los Angeles in 1926. The practice of using the Model AL six-cylinder engine in Bulldog-type fire apparatus, during 1926 and 1927, was dropped with the application of the complete AL chassis as Type 90 fire apparatus in 1928.[9] For fire service the AL engine was rated at over 100 hp, with a pumping capacity of 750 g.p.m.

Production of the traditional four-cylinder Bulldog fire engine was soon phased out with the rapid expansion of the six-cylinder fire apparatus line during 1927 and 1928. While the four-cylinder Mack AB bus chassis continued to find suitable application in fire and emergency service up to 1930, the need for greater speed and power caused most fire chiefs to specify six-cylinder engines in their new equipment by this time.

By the end of the summer of 1928 the new Mack Type 19 fire engine, using the AP engine, was ready for marketing. The Type 19 had a conventional radiator and hood configuration in place of the traditional Bulldog-type hood and cooling system, and replaced the Type 15. When first introduced, Type 19 pumpers were offered in 750 to 1,000 g. p. m. capacities and had dual reduction drive. However, some large AP powered pumpers and emergency squad trucks were built with the Bulldog-type hood and chain-drive for delivery to New York City in 1930 and 1931. It is believed these were the last Bulldog-type fire apparatus to be produced.

The year 1928 also saw the beginning of a concerted effort to introduce a line of conventional looking Mack trucks with high speed capabilities and four wheel brakes. The Model BJ marked

This Mack fire engine, built on the Model AL bus chassis, entered the service of the Indianapolis Fire Department in December 1927.

A side view from the rear shows the deck gun in a raised position and the straps for the firemen to hang on to as the AP sped to the scene of a fire. One of seven type 19's built in 1930 for the city of New York, and the last fire apparatus to be made with Bulldog hoods.

In 1927 Mack tested this prototype Model BJ, first of a series of conventional looking six-cylinder trucks.

Mack's first modern six-cylinder commercial truck chassis, being announced in the summer of 1928. When first introduced, the BJ used the Model AL engine, a four-speed transmission mounted amidships, and a dual reduction rear axle. The four wheel service brakes operated through a vacuum booster, and a deluxe cab was standard equipment.[10] Capacity was given as three to four tons, and the BJ was not recommended for dump truck service, as it was geared to provide fast highway service.

While chain-drive was not available in the new Model BJ Mack, another six-cylinder truck, the Model BC, was offered in both dual reduction and chain-drive versions. The BC was introduced late in 1929, and offered a capacity of 2-1/2 to three tons,[11] which was later raised to four to five tons. The BC had its own 100 brake horsepower engine. The radiator, sheet metal work, and cab designs made it look like an updated version of the Model AB truck. As a chain-drive dumper, the BC was built in a wheel-base of 154 inches, and while it may have taken some customers from the Model AB Mack, was a little too small to have affected Bulldog sales any. A Model BC bus chassis was also introduced in 1929, at which time the AL bus and engine were discontinued.

In an apparent effort to test the market for a Mack truck in the one to 1-1/2 ton capacity range, the Model BB was introduced in the fall of 1928.[12] The BB truck used the basic AB four-cylinder engine, had a low chassis height, special coupe cab, and four wheel brakes. While attracting a fair degree of buyer interest in 1928 and 1929, the BB was replaced late in 1929 by the Model BG, having a nominal 1-1/2 ton capacity. However, a few special BB units, with both four and six-cylinder engines were produced up to 1932. The BG Mack had vacuum assisted four wheel brakes and its own six-cylinder engine, which produced 75 horsepower at 2,600 rpm. The BG was quite successful, being built up to 1937. Another light-duty Mack, the Model BL of one ton capacity, introduced early in 1930, also had four wheel brakes and a relatively high-speed six-cylinder engine.[13]

An effort was also made to use the most efficient six-cylinder engine models in each Mack vehicle at this time. In 1929, the improved BK bus engine replaced the AL bus engine in the BJ truck and Type 90 fire apparatus, which was completely redesigned. The BK engine developed 110 hp at 1,700 rpm, while the AL engine was originally rated at 97 at 2,200 rpm, for a less efficient power plant according to Mack standards. Mack engine designers still proceeded on the principle that optimum engine life and efficiency was attainable by producing maximum horsepower at a moderate engine speed. The relatively low-speed, high horsepower concept was applied mainly to the largest Mack engines, where a high road speed was still not a major consideration in their application.

Mack's line of truck equipment, which included winches, dump bodies, and an under-body screw hoist, was continued on a steady basis during the late 1920s. Some custom-built bodies were also made, as before, at the Long Island City plant, but only on a limited basis. Unfortunately, little progress was evidenced by the light weight aluminum container for less-than-carload railroad shipments, and it was quietly discontinued by 1930.

During 1928 several improved full-trailer models, having power brakes, were readied for production. The four-wheeled five ton trailer used some AB truck components, such as axles and wheels. It was offered with either solid or pneumatic tires, and had a B-K vacuum booster brake as standard equipment. Another four-wheeled trailer was built in a 10 ton capacity, using some AK and AC truck parts. A large six-wheeled trailer of 12 to 15 tons

The Mack line of full-trailers included a few heavy-duty models using some components from the AC and AK trucks. This non-reversible four-wheel trailer uses the six-spoked AK rear wheels.

Two ACP rail cars being tested on the Philadelphia & Reading Railway in August 1925. The first ACP unit is a straight passenger car, and the second is a combination passenger and baggage.

capacity was also offered, and, because of its extra weight, used only solid tires. Air brakes were standard equipment on the six-wheeler, and some petroleum carriers preferred this type of trailer as a tanker to be pulled behind one of their Bulldog tank trucks.

The Mack rail car program, which had seen at least 22 Bulldog-type units produced between 1921 and 1925, seemed to shift emphasis to a heavier type car in the latter year. About three units of the new ACP model, which used a more standard looking railroad car body, were completed by Allentown and tested in the fall of 1925. The ACP used an AC engine in each rail-truck and a straight mechanical drive, with four forward and four reverse speeds. During the testing on a midwestern railroad one of the units developed a technical problem and was shipped back to Allentown for repairs. A decision was later made to use a gas-electric system of propulsion in the larger Mack rail cars, which caused the ACP model to be shelved.[14]

A new Mack rail car program was instituted at the Plainfield plant by 1927, with all rail units being of the gas-electric type. The basic power plant for the new AS, AR, and AQ rail cars was the AP engine mated to a large electric generator which produced current to drive traction motors in each car's rail-trucks. The Model AS had only one AP engine-generator set, while the AR had two

The newly developed AC "High Hat" engine was used to power the ACP rail car, with one engine in each railway truck. Here the inspection hatch in the car body's floor has been raised to view the top of the power plant.

Each ACP railway truck was a self contained power unit with engine, radiator, shaft drive, and special dual reduction drive to one axle. Each rail car had two such trucks.

Testing the new Model BR Special switching locomotive during the summer of 1928 at the Plainfield Plant.

The BR Special switcher was rated at 12 tons, and used two Bulldog hoods. Note the modified Mack Year 'Round truck cab.

sets, and the AQ was designed to take three sets. About 20 of the large units were built before the gas-electric rail car program was phased out during 1929.[15]

The two-engined and double-hooded Bulldog locomotive, built by the Allentown plant in 1921, must have served as an inspiration for the Plainfield plant to build a similar unit by 1928. The new Bulldog-type locomotive was of the gas-electric type, using only a single AC engine coupled to an electric generator, and was cooled by the basic Type V radiator. This locomotive was rated at a weight of 12 tons and was called the Model BR Special. Although the BR Special had two Bulldog hoods, one at each end, only one AC engine was used, and the second hood covered an air compressor and auxiliary equipment.

Plans were drawn for an even larger 18 ton Bulldog-type industrial locomotive using the AP engine, called the Model AV. However, it is doubtful if this model was ever built or if more than one BR Special was constructed, as switching locomotives of a more conventional railroad design were produced after 1928. The Mack Rail Car Department offered locomotives in 18, 30, 45, and 60 ton sizes, each having the AP engine and electric generator set, either singly or in multiples, depending on the size of the unit. A 12 ton model of conventional design, called the BR Standard, also used the AC engine. About 18 locomotives were built by Plainfield after 1927, with one being sold as late as 1937.[16]

A raised hood on one end of the BR Special exposed the AC engine. The engine was coupled to an electric generator for the traction motors, which actually propelled the locomotive. The generator and an air pump for the train brakes were housed under the other hood.

In expanding their commercial vehicle line to include a variety of light and medium-duty six-cylinder trucks, Mack management had not over-looked the need for additional muscle in their heavy truck models. The new line, comprising a new AP series of the Bulldog-type and six-wheeled units of both the AC and AP models, constituted the Super-Duty Mack models formally introduced during 1929.[17] That Chief Engineer A. F. Masury took a personal interest in the new Mack models, there can be little doubt, as the AP was shaped in the Bulldog image, and was a culmination of Masury's pioneering career in heavy truck construction.

Alfred Fellows Masury was born in Danvers, Massachusetts, on September 2, 1882, and later showed all the qualities of ingenuity and industry for which the pioneer New Englanders established such an enviable reputation. A. F. Masury was the son and only child of Charles H. and Evelyn (Fellows) Masury, who were direct descendants of John Endicott, governor of the Bay Colony during its founding in the 1600s. Alfred's father served as a captain in the Civil War, being wounded at the Battle of Bull Run. His father was also active in civil affairs until the time

This chassis, with the Model AP engine, is believed to be the prototype Prime Mover that Masury's staff had been working on as a possible military vehicle. Note new forged steel radius rod.

of his death, as was his mother, who belonged to such groups as the Daughters of the American Revloution and National Women's Suffrage Movement.[18]

Young Masury attended local public schools and later matriculated at Brown University in Providence, Rhode Island, where he graduated with a degree in mechanical engineering in 1904. His first full-time job was with the Lynn (Massachusetts) Works of the General Electric Company, where he served as a junior engineer during 1904 and 1905.[19] Masury was next employed by the Corwin Manufacturing Company, successors to the Vaughn Machine Company, Peabody, Massachusetts, which was known for its wide range of processing machinery for the leather working, textile, and printing industries. The reason he switched from the comparative security of a large corporation to a relatively small firm, which had just gone through a reorganization, may be deduced from his evident interest in the growing field of automotive design work.

The Vaughn Machine Company had started to build internal combustion engines and related automobile parts for some of the many small concerns which began the construction of pleasure cars in the early 1900s. Apparently by 1904, Vaughn had made arrangements to manufacture an automobile called the Gas-Au-Lec, and the English Coulthard steam truck. These projects were continued during 1905 and into 1906 by Corwin.[20]

The Gas-Au-Lec automobile was the invention of Ralph Hood of Danvers, Massachusetts. It had some very unusual features, such as a gearless transmission, auxiliary electric propulsion motor, and self-starter. Masury rendered assistance to Hood on some of the design work, and the fact that both men were from Danvers may have been the reason they collaborated in the first place. However, Hood would not agree to the substitution of mechanical valve lifters for a unique type of magnetic lifters that were malfunctioning due to the engine heat burning the insulation on the wiring of the electro-magnets, and the project fizzled out.[21] While the Gas-Au-Lec did not make it in the infant auto industry, Masury's interest in solving automotive design problems only grew with each new experience.

A. F. Masury was also involved with some design problems associated with the production of the Coulthard five ton steam truck. A Coulthard steam truck had won a gold medal for its comparatively good showing in the heavy truck group during the first Commercial Vehicle Contest held in New York City on May 20th and 21st, 1903.[22] Steel tires had been used, which evidently caused excessive vibrations as the truck proceeded over the cobble-stoned streets, causing the main steam line to fracture. Later, wooden block tires, made of maple, were substituted, but the truck itself was only marginally successful, being last advertised in the fall of 1906. While heavy steam trucks enjoyed a relatively long period of acceptance in England, possibly due to smoother road conditions, the American market was unresponsive and few were ever sold in the United States.

During his busy, but short, career with Corwin, Masury had established a fine reputation in the still struggling motor vehicle industry and was ready for a managerial position. This opportunity came in 1907, when E. R. Hewitt was seeking a factory manager for his Hewitt Motor Company, and was also preparing to market an expanded line of heavy truck models. In July 1907, Masury became one of the incorporators of the Hewitt Motor Truck Company, an affiliate of the Hewitt Motor Company, and was soon working out the details of a new 10 ton truck. Lacking adequate space in the New York factory, Masury supervised the construction of at least 20 of the 10 ton models by two outside contractors.

After the merger of the Hewitt Motor Company with the International Motor Company early in 1912, Masury served in important sales and service positions until becoming chief engineer of I. M. C. in the summer of 1914. Masury's collaboration with Hewitt in designing the outstanding AB and AC models was followed by his shrewd promotional ideas to demonstrate the great utility of the new trucks. A good example of this was the loaning of the AC prototype test truck, E-2, for the 1915 summer encampment of a U. S. Army training corps at Plattsburg, New York. This was followed early in 1916 by the building of several armored cars, some on AB models, for use by the New York State National Guard, with the cost of the work being donated by a private citizen.

With the United States' active participation in World War I, large orders for AC Macks, placed by the War Department, were quickly followed by special government projects. Masury supervised the design and construction of a mobile anit-aircraft gun carriage, and special AC searchlight truck with dual radiators and engine-driven generator for powering the searchlights. He also served as a technical advisor during the development of the standardized army truck for the Quartermaster Corps, although the International Company never built any of the so called "Liberty" trucks. Masury's continuing interest in the problems of applying the motor truck to military service, prompted his close association with the Army Ordnance Department, which helped test some of his ideas. In 1928 the Society of Automotive Engineers appointed Masury Chairman of the Army Ordnance Advisory Committee in recognition of his unselfish devotion to this important work.[23]

Following the conflict of 1914 - 1918, the Quartermaster Corps, which handled the major supply function of the U. S. Army, had been given the major responsibility for army motor transport. Naturally, other branches of the service as well as departments of the army used motor vehicles, but the Q. M. C. had a total of 17,305 vehicles by 1929, with 16,542 of these being of World War I vintage.[24] These vehicles were periodically

A direct front view of the huge Prime Mover presents an awesome sight. Note extreme length of radiator and Mack Safety League sticker on front bumper.

The Prime Mover after its sale to a petroleum company for tanker service in 1929. Note the triple rear tires.

The right-hand side of the huge AP engine showing intake manifold with the exhaust manifold directly over it.

Left-hand side of the AP engine shows the magneto ignition, and the large aluminum alloy heads that all new Mack engines received by the late 1920s.

overhauled at Camp Holabird, in Baltimore, Maryland, where a few experimental military trucks were also built, starting in the early 1920s. By 1928 a great need was evidenced by both the Q. M. C. and the Ordnance Department, which had charge of artillery, in obtaining motor trucks of increased power and improved performance that were suitable for military service. Specifically, Ordnance was interested in the development of a prime mover for hauling tanks and pulling large mobile howitzers.

In the fall of 1928 the Long Island City plant assembled an experimental truck chassis having the AP engine, and frontal placement of a large elongated radiator for a conventional looking heavy-duty truck. The cab, wheels, and chain-drive were identical to the largest 7-1/2 ton AC models, except for forged steel radius rods, most likely needed to take the extra power produced by the huge six-cylinder engine. It is believed that this vehicle was part of a prime mover project for the U. S. Army, but was sold in 1929 to a New York based petroleum company. A photographic record does exist which shows the AP chassis before and after the mounting of a tank body, as well as pulling a large four-wheeled tank trailer.

The first production version of the new Model AP turned out by Allentown early in 1929 was quite different in appearance from the 1928 AP test truck. A 13-louvered Bulldog-type hood and Type V cooling system were in the best Masury tradition of easy product identification. The Mack Year 'Round cab was used on the first group of AP trucks built, and in March and August several pneumatic tired AP's were completed for the U. S. Army. These were six-wheeled versions of the AP, with four-wheel, chain-drive bogies, and capable of carrying the army's light tank. Some of the army jobs had winches, but all were equipped with low-sided steel dump bodies.

The basic four-wheeled Model AP was designed to carry loads of 7-1/2 tons at speeds up to 30 mph. With the huge six-cylinder engine, rated at 150 horsepower at 2,000 rpm, powering the truck, sales literature claimed the new Mack could handle, "... trailer loads of any tonnage up to the tractive limit of two driving wheels, with modern high-speed performance."[25] The Mack AP truck had chain-drive and used the same basic drive system as the heaviest AC chassis. Since the huge engine would be very difficult, if not impossible, to hand-crank, an electric starter was standard equipment, as were vacuum brakes on the rear wheels.

The Super-Duty six-wheeled Mack AC and AP models were

First 1929 production AP truck had an extra-long Bulldog-type hood to cover the big six-cylinder engine. Note use of the Mack Year 'Round cab with sliding doors.

Carburetor side of AP engine shows the large tapered exhaust manifold over the smaller intake manifold.

Front view of AP engine showing cradled suspension, a traditional construction feature of the Bulldog Mack.

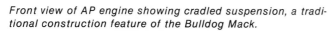

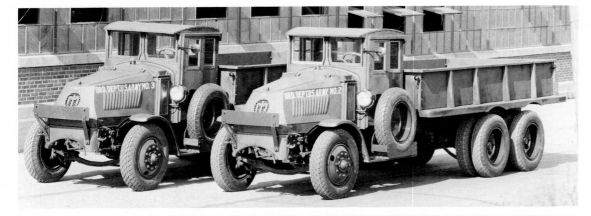

Two AP 10-ton capacity Army T2 prime movers, with the new Mack chain-drive bogie, purchased for the Army Ordnance Dept. in 1929.

Testing a two-wheel drive Mack bogie in 1926. The boxes of pig iron added up to at least a nine-ton load.

the result of several years of determined design and test work. Masury's interest in this work was acknowledged at the 1928 Annual Transportation Meeting of the Society of Automotive Engineers, where he appeared as chairman of the Six-Wheel Vehicle Design vs. Legislation symposium. The group's report included the many benefits claimed for six-wheelers from the operator's viewpoint, although not without some challenges, and concluded with the main point that states were beginning to legislate in favor of six-wheelers.[26] Many state laws restricting the weight of motor vehicles set a maximum weight that could be carried for each inch of tire width, regardless of the weight of the chassis. It logically followed: if truckers were to increase their

payloads per trip, more or wider tires would have to be added to their vehicles.

During the summer of 1926 a special long-framed Bulldog truck was equipped with a two-axle, four-wheeled tandem assembly at the rear, having chain-drive to the forward wheels of the tandem unit. Mack nomenclature soon called the tandem assembly a "bogie," which was from a British term originally used for a low, strongly built cart, and later associated with their four-wheeled railroad car-trucks. Rapid progress was then made on the design and testing of a Mack bogie that had chain-drive to all four wheels, as well as power brakes on the same wheels. The new Mack six-wheeler, 6 x 4, was based on the basic 4-Speeder

A top view of the 1926 six-wheeler shows the chain-drive going only to the forward wheels of the bogie unit.

Bulldog, and was previewed in the *Mack Bulldog* during the summer of 1927. In addition to the superior traction provided by the extra driving wheels, a third differential, called a Krohn Kompensator, proportioned the power between the two jackshafts, in order to avoid strains in the drive system.

Since both the AC and AP Super-Duty six-wheelers were rated at 7-1/2 to 10 tons capacity, the principal difference between them was the greater power and speed of the Model AP. Like the four-wheeled version, the six-wheeled AP could make sustained speeds of 30 mph with a full load, as well as climb a 20 percent grade. As a tractor it was rated to pull 35 ton trailer loads at 25 mph. The less powerful AC six-wheeler, rated at a capacity of also 7-1/2 to 10 tons, was credited with a top speed of 20 mph, and considered best adapted to work in congested areas where sustained speeds were not practical.

The bogie assembly of the AC and AP six-wheelers was essentially the same, and had several unique features. Power was not only equalized between each wheel by differentials in the hypoid-geared jackshafts, but a Mack Power Divider proportioned the power between the two jackshafts. The Power Divider was an adaptation of the Krohn Kompensator, acting as a differential under ordinary conditions, but transmitting torque to the wheels having traction when one wheel began to slip.[27] Differences in individual wheel travel occurred in bogies when the truck cornered, went over uneven road surfaces, or when new and used tires were not matched by their exact diameters. If differences in wheel travel were not equalized in a four-wheel drive bogie, some part of

Direct side view of a 1929 Bulldog dumper with balloon tires and four-wheel drive bogie. Mack had introduced a four-wheel drive bogie using chains to each wheel during the summer of 1927.

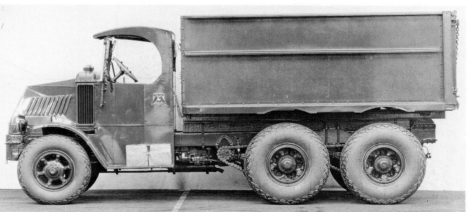

Elevated view of Mack chain-drive bogie shows use of special transmission and jackshafts. The four-wheel drive bogie, although costing more, gave far superior traction than the two-wheel drive bogie.

the drive assembly would be forced to bind or twist to absorb the uneven force, and often tires would skip in releasing the pent up energy.[28] Another important feature of the Mack bogie was hemispherical joints on the ends of the springs, which relieved lateral twisting of the spring leaves.

Despite the logic of the AP's ability to lower the unit delivered cost of various commodities, few were sold to the highway trucking industry. A scant number were tried in the bulk delivery of petroleum products and coal. The super power and chain-drive features of the AP did create interest in the construction industry, and it would be in the area of contracting that the AP would eventually prove its great value as a Super-Duty truck. Of course, the AP engine had already established itself in the fire apparatus field, but poor sales as a highway freighter were due to circumstances beyond the control of Masury and the Mack engineering staff.

Part of the problem was the much higher initial cost of the AP chassis, which probably created buyer resistance in the early depression years following 1929. As a super highway hauler, Mack promotional pieces pictured the AP as the six-wheel version, which would also be pulling a full trailer, resulting in a huge double payload. However, it is believed that restrictive motor vehicle weight and length laws in some states during the early 1930s, reversing a more liberal trend, helped to hurt sales of the big highway units. Unfortunately, even the U. S Army market faded due to a restrictive cost-per-vehicle stipulation placed in a large Congressional appropriation, enacted in 1931, which in turn caused the Quartermaster Corps to assemble their own trucks at Camp Holabird.[29]

The 4-Speeder's Final Form

While the late 1920s witnessed a decided decline in the sales of new Bulldog Macks, the truck's general popularity never

A typical 1929 Bulldog chassis with new forged steel radius rods. Note crown fenders which were introduced during 1927. Not shown is the one-piece windshield introduced in 1929.

Removable aluminum alloy heads of slightly unusual size prompted the nickname "High Hat" for the new AC engine, introduced in 1928 after a long trial period.

seemed greater, with new or more difficult applications a constant challenge to its fine reputation. Several important mechanical modifications were made to up-date the basic AC chassis, but these made little visible change in the truck's outer appearance. Also, several optional features were offered, some of which were easily recognizable, but all of which added to the Bulldog's performance and flexibility of service.

The improved AC engine, with two large removable heads and cylinders cast in a single block, instead of pair-cast, was introduced early in 1928. The heads were comparatively high, inspiring the nickname, "High Hat," among mechanics and heavy

truck users in general. It was stated that the aluminum heads were unusually large and held to the engine block by 15 studs in order to eliminate expansion troubles.[30] A redesigned combustion chamber, giving a higher compression ratio than the previous AC engine, was apparently used to take advantage of the improved regular grade of gasoline available by the late 1920s. Brake horsepower of the High Hat AC engine was given as 72 at 1,400 rpm.

One group of improved components involved the principle of inter-changeability, much desired in the automotive industry to help cut manufacturing costs and improve the general availability

Direct front view of new High Hat AC engine shows non-standard dual magneto and distributor ignition system. This type of dual ignition system was usually specified for fire apparatus.

Left-hand close-up of High Hat engine shows inspection ports, one with a combination oil filler and crankcase breather. The electric starter was optional extra equipment.

of service parts at a reasonable expense to the customer. The introduction of the Models AK and AP, the Bulldog look-alikes, was an opportunity to plan component designs with an eye to the compatibility of their function on improved versions of the AC, and vice versa. Examples of how this worked out were the use of the deeper AK cab on some AC models, starting about 1930, and the use by the AP and AC models of the forged steel radius rod, by the end of 1929. The pressed steel radius rod used on the AC was dropped at this time.

The growth in popularity of pneumatic tires, which had been available on special order on the 3-1/2 ton AC since the late World War I era, suddenly boomed during 1928 and 1929. Cast steel wheels, having six spokes each, were offered with the optional pneumatics during 1928. Budd steel disc wheels were also available, and these became popular on the Model AK by 1930. On the larger capacity Bulldogs a combination of pneumatics on the front wheels and solids on the rear became a compromise to help cushion the front end while avoiding the high cost of dual

Right-hand close-up of High Hat engine shows air cleaner and "stove pipe" to carry warmed air to the carburetor. The generator, to the front of the carburetor, is a non-standard component.

pneumatics on the rear. The regular steel spoked solid tired AC wheels had almost completely superseded the prior wooden wheels during the early 1920s. However, there were one or two commercial vehicle applications which continued to specify wooden wheels during the late 1920s.

The use of pneumatic tires, especially the improved balloon type, was so extensive by 1930 that the conversion of solids by truck owners became commonplace. Since it was impossible to just install pneumatics on wheels built to hold solids, due to the entirely different rim designs and inside tire diameters, two basic conversion methods were used. The first and simplest was the purchase of new wheels which were designed to take the desired size of pneumatic tire. The other method used, mostly in the 1930s, was called "Cut and Weld" and involved cutting off the ends of the steel spokes so that a felloe-band of a smaller diameter could then be welded on. This method sometimes necessitated the use of a large lathe to even-up the spoke ends so that the felloe could be mounted true on the wheel.

It should be noted that the AC was equipped with solid tires of a standard diameter, being 36 inches in front and 40 inches

The front wheels of this pre-1929 Bulldog have been converted from solids by cutting away the ends of the steel spokes and welding on new felloe-bands to take large pneumatic tires.

rear, except the tractor version which had carried 34 inches front and 36 inches rear since 1925. The width of the solid tires used varied with the capacity of the related AC chassis, being wider on the heavier units. Balloon-tired Bulldogs usually had the same size tires front and rear, with the use of duals on the rear wheels.

A device called a "hubodometer," to measure distance traveled, was installed in an elongated left front wheel hub on the Bulldog since about 1920. The hubodometer took the place of the odometer on a speedometer, which had not been supplied on the Bulldog. However, a dash-mounted odometer or a speedometer was available as extra equipment by 1930.

The importance of extra gear ratios, in addition to the changeable sprockets in the chain-drive system, was recognized by 1930 when two optional equipment items became available. A two-speed auxiliary transmission, with 1.00 and 1.94 to 1.00 ratios, could be installed between the clutch and standard four-speed AC transmission, providing eight speeds forward and two reverse. A special transmission, called the "7-2," providing seven forward speeds and two reverse, was available in place of the standard four-speed AC gearbox. The 7-2 transmission was provided with two sets of constant mesh gears and can not be con-

sidered a modified AC transmission. The added gear ratios were very important to many contractors, especially to those using pneumatic tired trucks which ran at a greater variety of high and low speeds than solid tired trucks in the same service.

There were several other optional items available on the Bulldog by 1930. The pneumatic-tired Bulldogs, with their higher road speeds, were soon offered with vacuum booster brakes for safer operation. However, vacuum and air brakes were also important with the use of tractors pulling the larger, balloon-tired trailers coming into vogue. Electric starting and lighting, or lighting systems alone, gained in popularity, although mostly in Bulldogs used in highway service.

Several expanded roles for the Bulldog in the construction industry are worthy of note. The concept of delivering freshly mixed concrete to construction sites by truck, rather than mixing it with expensive equipment restricted to one site, grew quickly after the development of the proper truck equipment. By 1929 several construction equipment manufacturers were producing revolving mixer bodies, and the Bulldog was again called upon to demonstrate its ability to successfully handle a tough new assignment. The Model AC was selected because the heavy-duty

A 1928 pneumatic-tired Bulldog with Budd disc wheels loading heavy concrete sewer pipe with the aid of a Mead-Morrison horizontal boom.

Early 1929 Bulldog concrete mixer truck in full-discharge position. Note use of the Wood hydraulic-cable hoist.

Introduction of truck-mounted concrete mixers by the late 1920s was a boon to the construction industry. The Bulldog's wide frame, chain-drive, and super strength construction, were features that were a perfect match for the new service.

construction and extra width of its frame were ideal for the mounting of heavy machinery.

The late 1920s saw improved cranes and power shovels being mounted on the AC Mack, and even attachments to keep the wheels from bogging down in excavation sites. The Browning Crane and Shovel Company selected the Bulldog Mack for use with its truck mounted power shovel, having a 1/2-yard dipper, 14 foot dipper stick, and 18 foot boom. The Christie Crawler track laying attachment for crane trucks was perfected by 1927, and used mainly by contractors needing extra traction and floatation for their equipment during its use on soft ground. Heavy oil well servicing equipment, such as large pumps and draw-works were mounted on Bulldogs, many of which spent 20, 30, or even over 40 years in the oil fields of the Southwest and California.

By the late 1920s Bulldog tractors in the construction industry were also pulling I-beam trailers, with some of the largest types of cranes and power shovels straddling a very narrow and low type of trailer bed. Some contractors liked the I-beam trailer because it was generally easy to load, and the equipment carried

on them presented a safe, low center of gravity. However, while they also provided a better clearance for over-head obstructions, ground clearance for the overhanging crawler treads of a power shovel on board was very minimal, and the loaded trailer had difficulty going over some sharp road grades, such as railroad crossings.

Bulldog tractors remained popular during the late 1920s, especially in the field of heavy hauling. Built in a basic 128 inch wheelbase, they were offered in three capacities by 1930: 7-10 ton, 11-14 ton, and 15 ton. Some truckers preferred the Year 'Round cab, as it gave drivers better protection from the elements. On the other hand, most heavy haulers preferred the traditional covered cab for greater driver visibility and ease of access. However, a few heavy equipment haulers liked the open cab, as it allowed the boom of a crane, loaded on a low bed trailer behind the tractor, to extend out in front of the tractor at a relatively low level. There was also a special narrow cab available for trucks used for hauling long lengths of pipe, which allowed part of the load to extend past the cab to the front of the truck.

A Christie Crawler-equipped Bulldog crane with clamshell bucket loading a Pierce-Arrow dumper. The worm-drive Pierce was quite popular in the building supply industry, but faded from production about 1933.

A Christie Crawler attachment was a definite asset to a Bulldog-mounted crane when traveling over soft ground. The crawler track was usually removed for ordinary street operation.

Heavy hauling contractors in the Cleveland area liked the Bulldog with open cab. This 1927 AC is pulling a Rogers gooseneck semi-trailer loaded with a huge crawler-mounted paver, used in road construction.

A St. Louis contractor hauls an Erie crawler equipped crane on a low-bed full-trailer. Note extended body floor around special narrow cab and front-mounted pipe rack, for carrying extra length pipe on the early 1929 Bulldog.

Moving a huge tunnel shield used in New York subway construction, and weighing 163 tons. Such shields were used to push tunnel work through river beds and in places were the "cut and cover" method was considered objectionable.

Many American circuses used Bulldog Macks to provide a variety of services. Here a 1928 vintage Bulldog with water tank gives a cooling bath to the elephants.

This pre-1927 Bulldog with water tank was used by a large traveling carnival up to the World War II period. Note large lug tires on rear wheels to gain traction on the lots used by the show.

Bulldog six-wheelers were also built in the 6 x 2 version, in addition to the 6 x 4 Super-Duty type. Providing traction to only two rear wheels of a six-wheeler was apparently not a drawback to such a truck's performance where road conditions were favorable. However, Mack sales literature stressed the importance of having power supplied to all four rear wheels of a six-wheeler, and production records indicate that few of the 6 x 2 Bulldogs were built up to 1931. Such trucks were used for mostly general hauling in urban areas, and the majority of 6 x 2 Bulldogs were not factory built, but the result of third axle conversions in the field.

An unusual type of service for the Bulldog was its use with circuses, carnivals, and wild west shows. At least five circuses had short wheel-based 4-Speeder AC's by the late 1920s, and two wild west shows and a carnival were also using Bulldogs by 1930. Circus Bulldogs were used as stake drivers for the big top, and as tank wagons for watering down the elephants and other stock. They also provided water for the cook house, performers, and for vital fire fighting purposes. Other jobs for the circus Bulldogs were: pulling wagons to and from the lot, loading them on railroad flat cars, and often adding the grand finale by pulling the steam calliope at the end of the street parade. Many circus AC's were used up to the 1950s, and at least one carnival had them in the early 1960s.

Flying High with Mack and Masury

The late 'twenties were a time of rapid progress in the truck industry, with most manufacturers enjoying several years of relative prosperity following a recession in 1927, which hit some firms rather hard. Mack product strategy quickly shifted to the development of six-cylinder truck models after 1927, and the company remained quite profitable until the depression of the 1930s restricted sales to an ever increasing extent. During this period, Chief Engineer Masury showed there was practically no limit to the scope of his interests in the engineering field, creating a mild sensation by his presence aboard the Graf Zeppelin when it attempted a transatlantic flight in 1929. Masury's continuing role in Mack engineering developments was highlighted by a wide variety of experimental vehicles, some of which had the unmistakable likeness of his beloved Bulldog truck.

This Bulldog bringing the Big Top canvas and poles to the lot replaced 24 horses. Picture taken in 1937.

The steam calliope was usually the last unit in the circus parade, being pulled by the faithful Bulldog. Note boy holding his ears against the strident notes of the calliope, and baby elephant just ahead of the AC.

Total U. S. truck sales during 1927 dropped to 464,793 from the record level of 608,617 the year before.[31] Mack's plant shipments of commercial vehicles fell to a level between those recorded in 1923 and 1924, which in turn restricted profits somewhat. A rapid recovery was evidenced in the industry as a whole, with factory sales rising to a record level of 881,909 trucks in 1929.[32] However, heavy-duty truck sales may not have par-

113

ticipated fully in the sales recovery, as deliveries of new Model AC trucks continued at a level only 50 percent of that recorded prior to 1927, according to company production figures. Production of AB trucks returned to the 1926 level by 1928, and only eased slightly in 1929, after the introduction of improved Mack truck models of similar capacities.

Profit levels remained good for Mack Trucks, Inc., during the late 1920s, as efficiently run factories and well trained sales and service forces made their contributions to the well being of the orgnization. Also contributing to the company's stability was a conservative financial policy which saw the redemption of all preferred stocks and accrued dividends, totaling $18 million, in 1929.[33] This was followed by the retirement of all outstanding loans, which made Mack completely debt free at the end of 1930. During 1927 a net of $5.8 million was achieved on sales of $55.3 million,[34] for a return of slightly better than 10 percent. Sales rose to $57.2 million in 1929 with a net profit of $6.8 million,[35] for a near 12 percent profit margin on sales.

Advertising and sales promotion activities were continued at a good level in the late 1920s, with the major thrust of Mack advertising directed at many important market areas. Elaborate sales booklets were prepared on about a dozen prime industries. Starting in 1927 the house organ, *Mack Bulldog*, was continued in a pocket size format. Early in 1930 a large New York City show room was opened in the Grand Central Station area, at which about two dozen Mack vehicles were displayed. In the first few months over 300,000 visitors viewed the exhibition, which included every basic Mack truck and bus model and even some examples of Mack fire apparatus and gas-electric locomotives.[36]

By 1930 a well-balanced line of Mack commercial vehicles had been achieved with the adding of three light and medium-duty six-cylinder models, having modern styling, to the AB and AC models with their more traditional construction features and design.

A. F. Masury, while being an automotive engineer by profession, was just as much an inventor or scientist, as evidenced by his keen interest in all the associated fields which he came in contact with while performing his duties at the International Motor Company. The extensive use of heavy trucks and related equipment in road building, as well as their use on highways, prompted Masury to take a special course in highway construction at Columbia University in New York City. Masury's interest in civil engineering grew with the contacts he made through his studies, and thereafter he kept up memberships in four organizations involved with highway design or construction work.[37]

It was only natural for Masury to be especially active with the Society of Automotive Engineers, serving on various committees during the mid-1920s, including the Diesel Engine Activity Committee. During World War I, his supervision of the design of the special Bulldog trucks with self-contained searchlight equipment and anti-aircraft gun-mount trailers for the air defense arm of the Army Corps of Engineers, added another dimension to a growing list of Masury's interests: Aviation. He became an ardent advocate of aviation, using it for transport purposes. The development of the huge dirigible-type airships had a particular fascina-

Mack entered the late 1920s with a wide variety of transportation products and a great background, as this large billboard indicates.

Mack Chief Engineer A. F. Masury had become deeply interested in airship development during the 1920s. Here Masury poses in front of the Goodyear blimp, Mayflower, late in 1929.

An inspection trip to Europe in 1929 brought Masury to the Bussing Works in Brunswick, Germany, and a look at a huge six-wheel Bussing test chassis. Masury is flanked by two Bussing officials, with the test driver on the extreme right, and Mack staff engineer, Gottfried Wirrer, seated behind the wheel.

tion for him, and it is believed he was able to fly on the U. S. S. Shenandoah[38] before it crashed in a storm in 1925.

In the spring of 1929 Masury and at least one other Mack engineer sailed for Europe to visit the facilities of several foreign automotive concerns.[39] Along on the inspection trip was Gottfried Wirrer, a highly skilled engineer of Swiss birth, who had entered the employ of the International Motor Company with its formation as a merger of the Mack Brothers Motor Car Company and Saurer Motor Company in 1911. Wirrer's original job with the firm of Adolph Saurer, A. G., of Arbon, Switzerland, had led to his coming to the United States to help set up production of Saurer trucks by the American licensee.

Wirrer developed a keen interest in machine tools and fathered 20 patented inventions related to critical production processes. No doubt Wirrer's knowledge of German and French, as well as his exacting grasp of precision production techniques, were a big help in Masury's discussions with the foreign automotive officials. While in Germany they visited manufacturers of diesel engines and six-wheeled commercial vehicles, on which designs European engineers had made great progress.

Upon completion of the inspection trip, Masury tried to return to America aboard the famous German airship Graf Zeppelin (Count Zeppelin), but after taking off from Friedrichshafen, Germany, on May 16, 1929, the craft was forced back due to severe buffeting and engine trouble encountered over Spain. Despite the problems witnessed during his aborted flight, Masury had only praise for the airship's commander, Dr. Hugo Eckener, and his highly disciplined crew. Masury wrote a special report on his dirigible flight for the S. A. E., covering in great detail the various technical aspects of the airship.[40]

Experimental work was very important to the future progress of the Mack product line, and the engineers tackled this task on a very broad front during the late 1920s. The Bulldog Mack's instant

Post card mailed by Masury during the aborted Graf Zeppelin transatlantic trip in May 1929. This card was sent to the late Harry Whitely, Captain of Masury's yacht, L'Apache.

An AB truck chassis fitted out with Bulldog-inspired hood in the summer of 1927.

public product recognition was of incalculable advertising value, and continued to prompt the use of similar sheet metal designs in some prototype vehicles with the hope that a possible new model would continue the noble tradition. During 1927 a Model AB truck was restyled with a Bulldog-like hood, but with a frontal radiator fitted in a slanting position, somewhat like the Model AL's radiator arrangement.

In 1928 Long Island City experimented with the E-63 test truck, an unusually low-slung six-wheeled chassis having a Bulldog hood and cooling system. Dual jackshafts provided chain-drive to all four rear wheels, and the drop-center axles provided extra flexing space for the highly arched transverse helper springs.

Late in 1930 a rather modernistic looking, for its day, cab-over-engine, chain-drive truck, obviously using a Bulldog chassis, was completed by the Long Island City plant. This unusual prototype c. o. e. Mack was designated the "AFM," most likely because of its cab which was shaped like a huge Bulldog hood,

and its ornamental front grill work which was also designed in the likeness of a direct front view of Masury's favorite truck.

Work on several other vehicle design concepts was started in the late 1920s, some of which would have an important bearing on future Mack products. In 1928 an AB chain-drive truck chassis was equipped with single motor electric drive, in an effort to eliminate the use of a standard mechanical transmission. Such gas-electric systems have achieved recurrent vogues of interest since the early 1900s, but only in very limited applications have they proven of any sustained value. Both AB and AL buses were available with a Mack designed gas-electric drive, but only about 200 of these were produced during the 1926 to 1928 period.

Raised hood of Model AB reveals slanting front-mounted radiator.

The E-63 test chassis was an attempt to provide a lower frame height and simplified bogie design for six-wheelers.

Rear view of the E-63 test chassis shows drop center axles, transverse helper springs, and lower frame height.

Close-up of the double jackshaft chain-drive bogie with light weight Budd steel disc wheels.

The 1930 AFM cab-over-engine test truck was obviously named after Mack's chief engineer. Note shape of cab is similar to the Bulldog's hood.

Side view of the AFM was taken at Allentown, before shipment to New York for finishing touches. Chain-drive and heavy construction indicates that a Bulldog chassis was used.

Also in 1928, Long Island City began work on two six-wheeled transit-type motor buses, having rear engines and integrated chassis and body frame construction. Photos have been found showing these buses during construction, but disposition of the test vehicles on completion remains a mystery. The rear-engine gas-electric design might have proved trouble-some, as the first transit-type Mack bus readied for production in 1931, called the Model BT, had its engine placed at the front of the body. Also, the first rear-engined Mack buses did not go into production until 1934.

The most important experimental work undertaken during the late 1920s was the development of a compression-ignition engine, commonly called a "diesel," after its inventor, Rudolph Diesel. The European trip made by Masury and Wirrer, in 1929, was directly involved with Mack's future production of its own diesel engine. However, at this stage in the project a tremendous

An AB truck chassis was converted to gas-electric propulsion early in 1928. A similar form of drive was offered on AB and AL buses, but did not prove very popular.

This view of the gas-electric shows electric motor drive to the jackshaft, via two U-joints, and the controller for speed control, next to the driver's seat.

amount of experimental work had to be done, with the obvious goal of giving the Mack diesel engine unique and patented design features. Mack's former chief engineer and long-time consultant, E. R. Hewitt, also traveled to Europe and participated in the research work. A Mercedes diesel engine was imported by 1931 and tested in a Model BC bus chassis, but the deepening depression of the 1930s no doubt restricted funding of the research efforts to some degree.

The main engineering department of the International Motor Company, which had been located on the top floor of the Long Island City plant after its move from 64th Street, was broken up in 1928. A. F. Masury moved his staff of experimental and special assignment engineers to the Mack executive offices at 25 Broadway, New York City.[41] Most, if not all, of the basic vehicle experimental work continued at Long Island City, where it could be closely supervised by Masury. The engineers working on the detail designs of regular production vehicles and components, after their approval by the Product Committee, were shifted to the respective plants producing them.

Engineers making the detail drawings of vehicles went to Allentown, those working on engines to Plainfield, and those designing geared components to New Brunswick. These plants had always maintained small engineering staffs to adapt various parts to specific manufacturing processes, but now they acquired more responsibility for complete vehicle and component designs. Chief Engineer Masury then had the task of visiting the plants to check and approve the new designs on a regular basis. It is believed that Allentown completed the engineering and prototype test vehicles for the new BG and BC truck models, introduced late in 1929.

Several important additions and changes were made to the Allentown and Plainfield plants, which helped to keep the Mack product line in a competitive position as the company faced the difficult depression years. The huge single story factory building, Plant 5C, which was located near Allentown's Plant 5, the shipping and storage center, had been used mainly for storing new buses since its completion in 1926. However, during 1928 5C took on the bus body, truck cab, and fire aparatus equipment lines, and had huge paint booths through which completed vehicles passed. At Plainfield the large Pond plant, of the Niles-Bement-Pond Company, was purchased in 1926 and made a vital part of the service parts function.

At Allentown the method of chassis construction was completely changed in 1926, with the setting up of chain-assembly and painting lines at Plants 4 and 4A, respectively. Prior to this time AB and AC trucks had been built at fixed positions, with the frames set on wooden horses. Parts were taken from the stock rooms, placed in suitable locations beside the frames, and gangs traveled from truck to truck, attaching components according to their specialized training. The assembly crews had to work efficiently, as each chassis had its allotted time in which to be completed.[42] Under the new system, which is basically still in effect, the frames pass slowly by various stations, to which the proper parts are routed and at which trained crews install their own particular components. A construction record accompanies each chassis, giving full details as to customer, model, chassis number, and the specific components to be used.

Along with the improved production setup, a new chassis numbering system was instituted at the end of 1929, which used a code prefixed to the actual chassis number indicating the basic component configuration in addition to the model designation.

Inside view of Allentown's huge Plant 5C shows several large AP fire engines in process of body construction during the summer of 1928.

Plant 5C later became Mack's bus assembly facility and contained huge paint spraying booths to aid in this work.

The number "4" or "6" came first in the code, indicating a four or six-cylinder engine. Then the letters designating the model, such as AB, AC, or BG, came next. Following the model designation was any one of a series of numbers, 1 through 8, each signifying an important characteristic of the chassis. Number "1" indicated a four-wheeled chassis; "2" a six-wheeler, with four-wheel drive bogie; "3" a mechanical-drive bus chassis, and so forth. A letter designation then followed, which was either "C" or "S," indicating the chassis used either chain or shaft drive.

Finally, on the AC, a system of three letters then followed: "L," "M," or "H," indicating which of the three capacity types the chassis represented: Light, Meduim, or Heavy. These capacity types corresponded to the 3-1/2, 5 to 6-1/2, and 7-1/2 ton Bulldog versions. The first four-cylinder Bulldog Mack of 7-1/2 tons capacity produced under the new system had the following chassis number: 4AC1CH1001. It should be noted that the letter "H" also indicated a heavy axle on other Mack truck models.

The old chassis numbering system for the AB and AC models, started during 1916 and 1917, used one or two digits at the beginning of the number to indicate the capacity of the chassis in thousands of pounds. Numbers beginning with "4" meant the chassis was rated at 4,000 pounds capacity, and a "13" indicated a 13,000 pound capacity, or two and 6-1/2 tons, respectively. Since the carrying capacities of the AB and AC models did not overlap, there was no conflict in the system until 1928 when the light and medium capacity six-cylinder Mack trucks were introduced. Also, the only exceptions to the system, prior to 1928, were the tractor versions which were numbered into their corresponding conventional truck models, and some special products like rail cars.

The reality of all the changes in the engineering and factory setups was to gear up the Mack organization to produce a wider variety of commercial vehicles being demanded by a market of growing divergence and sophistication. Even the traditional four-cylinder Bulldog, and its companion AK and AP models would come under the influence of the changing markets. A line of "Super Bulldogs" would soon be ready to meet the challenges of American's worst depression era which followed quickly on the heels of the stock market crash late in 1929.

Hauling zinc ore to the crusher in an open pit mine. These Bulldogs have heavy-duty side dump bodies.

Unloading the Bulldogs was a simple operation for one man with a winch and A-frame boom used to tip over the side-dump bodies.

Hitting The Highway

The Great Depression of the 1930s climaxed an era of great industrial expansion, wide-spread financial speculation, and swift technological changes. Although several million people became unemployed by 1931, following the stock market crash in the fall of 1929, the effects of the Depression on the basic economics of the country created various counter-currents, so that not all industries suffered equally; and not necessarily all firms in a given industry, for that matter. One interesting facet of the Depression era of the 1930s was the continued pace of technological changes in the face of severely curtailed industrial expansion and financial investment.

The automotive industry is a prime example of the continued need for technological improvements in product design despite the severe restrictions placed on capital formation due to very low profit margins. Trends in truck design, such as larger and more powerful engines, continued along with higher speed capabilities. The Bulldog Mack and its companion model, the AK, evidenced some important changes, which included six-cylinder models, improved six-wheelers, and adoption of balloon tires as a basic component in new chassis designs.

The big trend toward six-cylinder engines in the late 1920s became an overwhelming fact sooner than expected, with over 75 percent of all truck models finally having this type of engine by the end of 1930.[1] There were even a few examples of Straight-8 trucks at this time, but the standard truck engines had become the six-cylinder type due to its greater power and basic balance of design characteristics over the basic four-cylinder engine. By the end of 1930, the new six-cylinder AC and AK models were ready for introduction, along with other features which were compatible to both models.

The new six-cylinder Bulldog, designated as the Model AC-6, utilized the basic BK bus engine, which was adapted to the

The first pneumatic-tired AC-6 Bulldogs had the small crown fenders used on the AC-4 since about 1927. This AC-6 tractor started serving the Philadelphia area in the spring of 1931.

The BK bus engine was adapted to fit the Bulldog's Type V cooling system during 1930. However, this more powerful BQ engine was also adapted, and substituted for the BK engine by the end of 1932 in both the AC-6 and AK-6.

Bulldog's cooling system. With vacuum booster brakes on all four wheels, and balloon tires as standard equipment, the more powerful Bulldog attracted the interest of highway haulers whose needs combined both high tonnage and speed in delivery. During 1931 several over-the-road trucking concerns purchased AC-6 tractors for use with general merchandise trailers. Contractors and other local heavy haulers were especially attracted to the new Bulldog which was built in the six to nine tons capacity range as a four-wheeler. The AC-6 was only built in medium (M) and heavy (H) capacity designations, and did not compete against the light (L) capacity AC-4.

The importance of six-wheelers continued to grow right through the early 1930s, and a six-wheel Bulldog in the AC-6 series was introduced by early 1931. The new Bulldog six-wheeler used the basic four-wheel chain-drive Mack bogie, having the patented Power-Divider and medium-duty (M) rear axles.

Being designed as a basically balloon-tired, high-speed highway truck, certain important features were incorporated in the new six-wheel AC. As with the standard chain-drive Mack bogie, no jackshaft brakes were used, and all normal service braking was by vacuum assisted brakes in the front and rear wheels. An emergency, or parking brake, of the disc-type was attached to the propeller shaft. Larger, crown-type, front fenders were employed which were more suitable for the broader balloon

Huge six-wheel, AC-6 Bulldog and Mack six-wheel full-trailer were delivered in the fall of 1931. Combination was equipped with air brakes for improved driver control of the unit at high speeds.

tires than the previous narrower fenders, which had been designed for use with the standard solid tires of the AC-4's.

During 1931 and 1932 respectively, one AC-4 and one AC-6 six-wheeler with non-powered attachment axle were also constructed, most likely as experiments. It should be noted at this point that the use of attachment axles, also called "third" or "tag-axles," had taken on new meaning with the depression-economics of the early 1930s. Their use as a means for achieving legal axle-load limits with existing heavy-duty trucks during the late 1920s was broadened to include the boosting in capacity of light to medium-duty trucks at a relatively low cost.

Many companies entered the attachment axle business by the early 1930s with the attendant result that auto companies, which were also volume producers of light-duty trucks, then became a factor in the medium and relatively heavy-duty truck markets. The basically low-volume custom truck builders specializing in the medium and heavy-duty models, such as Autocar, Mack, and White, as well as many small regional producers, were adversely effected by this technological development. And while independent truck owners were more likely to buy a truck with an attachment axle due to the lower initial cost, some of the larger fleet operators also started to purchase such equipment, driven by the pressure to restrict capital expenditures. Consequently, Mack sales of six-wheel units were relatively small during the early 1930s, despite the noble attempt to offer a truck of balanced design that was more than a match for its intended service area.

This early 1931 AC-6, six-wheeler, with Heil eight-cubic yard dump body, has some unusual features. Note use of single tires on bogie, headlights mounted at cowl, and new Mack nameplate on hood.

An important step in Mack product strategy at this time was a continued rationalization of component use among various truck models, so as to effect production economies and increase service parts availability. The new AC-6 models used the AK front end, which included the rubber shock insulator system in the

Model AK-4, with Christie attachment axle, dumping coal at a Pennsylvania mine tipple. Many Macks were used in strip mining operations, starting in the early 1930s.

Model AK-4 having Christie attachment axle with drive chains running between the dual tires for improved traction. This unit served a Pennsylvania strip mine operation, starting in 1931.

spring brackets. Heretofore, the standard Bulldog series did not have this feature, but apparently a new, heavier version of the rubber block insert and steel bracket assemblies was devised. The AC-6 also used the larger AK covered cab, but coupe and some enclosed types of custom cabs became popular with the six-cylinder Bulldog, especially in over-the-road service.

Some important changes were also made in the Mack AK series for 1931. With the design of a new front end and dual reduction rear axle the original capacity rating of 3-1/2 to five tons, for the four-cylinder model, was raised to five to eight tons. Chain-drive was still offered with the AK-4, although the engine and combined transmission and jackshaft continued to be designated as Model AC components. The AK-4 was offered for essentially the same service as the AC-4 light-duty model, which was also raised from its former capacity rating.

The changes in the ratings for the AC-4 models during 1931 were most likely made in recognition of the fact that improved axle and radius rod components were being used by 1929. The higher ratings also recognized the heavy-service market that the Bulldog was selling in by 1930. New AC-4 capacities were

publicized in 1932 as: Light, five to eight tons; Medium, six to nine tons; and Heavy, seven to 10 tons.

No basic changes in AC-4 components were made during the 1932 to 1934 period, with the same optional equipment offered in 1929 being available for the most part up to 1934. A simple leaf-spring connection between each side rail and the front of each radius rod provided "flexible radius rods" by 1931, being furnished mostly on dump trucks bought by contractors. However, the "flexible radius rod" concept had its greatest impact in the huge off-highway AP models being developed in 1931, and will be covered in a description of the Super-Duty Macks that were designed for the famous Boulder Dam project.

The Mack BK six-cylinder engine was also used in the new Model AK-6 which was offered as a dual reduction version of the six-cylinder Bulldog. Only a few chain-drive units of the AK-6 were built in 1930, along with the first shaft-drive production units. A new spring hanger design was used in order to reduce the overall width of the rear end, so that a 96 inch width limit could be achieved while using balloon tires. Although able to attain speeds of up to 40 mph while fully loaded, the AK-6 was con-

Direct side view of 1931 AC-4 chassis shows installation of optional extra "flexible radius rod" device, used mainly on dump trucks.

sidered more of a lugger than a speed truck. The new six-cylinder AK had the same tonnage rating as the new AK-4; five to eight tons, and quickly found favor in both the general haulage and construction fields.

Utilizing the Mack dual reduction drive design, a new four-wheel drive bogie was developed for the AK-6 and introduced in 1931. Again, the capacity of the AK-6, six-wheeler, was comparable to the AC-6, six-wheeler, being eight to 15 tons. The new AK six-wheeler found some favor in the contracting and building supply fields but the Depression, which severely restricted new construction, also restricted sales of this and other new heavy-duty Mack models.

Despite the crushing effect that the Great Depression was having on new construction and other types of capital spending, certain important projects planned prior to the 1929 stock market crash were being pushed to conclusion during the early 1930s. It was reported that 100 Macks were being employed in 1931 to remove two million yards of fill (excavated material) from the site of the George Washington Bridge approaches.[2] And just as the famous Hudson River crossing was nearing completion, another major construction project of huge proportions in New York City was going through its first phases.

In Manhattan during the summer of 1931, excavation of the site for the foundations for the first buildings in the Rockefeller

Close-up of 1931 Bulldog chain-drive setup shows leaf-spring used in flexible radius rod installation. Note massiveness of radius rod, and shock insulated bracket for radius rod spring, above the radius rod.

Center complex was begun. It was completed in October 1932. As on the George Washington Bridge job, about 100 Macks were employed by the contractors charged with the removal of the rock and building rubble from the job site. All of the material had to be trucked out of the excavations, through busy mid-town vehicular and pedestrian traffic, mostly to piers for further

A typical AC-4 dumper of 1932 vintage with one-piece wind-shield and flexible radius rod device.

Close-up of two-wheel drive Mack bogie on AK-6 shows shaft-drive to only the forward bogie axle.

A long wheel-based AK-6 chassis with two-wheel drive Mack bogie developed in 1931.

Removing overburden in a Pennsylvania strip mine with the use of 1931 four-cylinder Bulldogs and a Lorain 75A power shovel. The coal seam can be seen in the foreground at the extreme left.

The foundations for the Rockefeller Center buildings, in New York City, required the tedious removal of over one million tons of rock and other materials. Bulldog Macks handled this work, which was accomplished during 1931.

Construction of Henry Hudson Parkway near the New York side of the George Washington Bridge in 1937. The Bulldog is a 1931 model, possibly converted from solid tires.

Most Rockefeller Center buildings were completed during 1932. These Bulldogs are waiting in front of the RCA Building, where the Christmas tree is erected annually.

transport by barge to final disposal sites. It is interesting to note that an estimated 1,338,000 tons of material were removed to make way for the new buildings, which were believed to weigh a total of 917,000 tons.[3] Both the old and new material was carried on the backs of heavy-duty trucks, with the Bulldog playing the predominant role in the combined operations.

Although the Bulldog and its companion models suffered a severe curtailment in production, with the output of AC, AK, and AP units during 1931 cut by more than half since 1929, Mack management had far from given up on the Bulldog's famous image. A new black enamel nameplate was designed in the shape of an elongated Bulldog hood, when the hood was viewed directly from the front. It first appeared in 1931 on the hoods of the B series Macks, and was described as being, "Cast in the Bulldog mold."[4]

After 1929, advertising budgets were restricted because of low profit margins. Only three issues of the *Mack Bulldog* house organ appeared during 1930, and two in 1931 before its suspension that year. At least one issue of a tabloid-sized four-page publication, *Mack Transport News*, was distributed during 1932, and a regular Mack house organ was not published again for many years. The popular *Mack Bulldog* magazine served its plea-sant purpose of colorfully illustrating the exploits of the Mack AC truck and its youthful admirer, Mickey. However, the realities of the Depression dictated tight budgets and struggling enterprizes had to put many frills aside for the duration.

Meeting A Bold Challenge

The increasing need to find jobs for the growing army of unemployed Americans finally focused on the concept of creating public works projects. National attention had been especially attracted to the spectacular Boulder Dam project, which seemed to reinspire confidence in the basic American ability to overcome great obstacles to accomplish a difficult task. The huge construction project astride the lower Colorado River on the Arizona-Nevada border provided a signal challenge, not only to the men employed but to all the equipment manufacturers wishing to participate in the needed business.

Seeing a tremendous opportunity to demonstrate Mack's ability to design and build a truck to meet the rugged job requirements, Chief Engineer Masury visited the dam site several times prior to the actual start of construction during the summer of 1931. He witnessed conditions which must have caused many

Early 1930s AK-6 service truck used by Mack's Bronx Branch. A clever design gave vehicle capability to both tow disabled trucks and stow heavy components in its body.

Black Canyon, on the Arizona-Nevada border, was the site of the huge Boulder Dam project, later renamed Hoover Dam. This 1932 view shows the Colorado River just before it was diverted through tunnels at the dam site.

observers to doubt the feasibility of the whole project as it was envisioned.

Steep walls of stone, some almost a thousand feet high, made up the Black Canyon dam site. A road had to be cut along the canyon walls so that trucks could reach the very bottom of the river bed, to begin removing material so that the foundation of the dam could be started. However, before excavations could start at the bottom, water tunnels had to be cut through the canyon walls, so that the river, blocked by coffer dams, could be diverted around the construction site. The time schedule called for equipment to run 24 hours a day, and seasonal temperatures, which ranged from about zero in the winter to over 110 in the shade during the summer, could not be allowed to halt the equipment.

A. F. Masury and his New York engineering staff quickly went to work on the assignment. An experimental unit, based on the Model AP, was developed to meet the problems envisioned. Because of the excessive heat of the area, as well as strenuous service to be performed, increased cooling capacity was achieved by placing an extra radiator at the front of the vehicle.[5] However, the dual radiator idea was soon abandoned in favor of an enlarged version of the traditional Bulldog-type, cowl-mounted radiator, and wire screening replaced the louvers in the

Production version of the special AP dump truck chassis developed for the boulder Dam project. Note extra wide radiator and air reservoir tanks for the powerful air brake system.

A rear view of the Boulder Dam AP chassis clearly shows under-slung rear springs and "Crow's Nest" for driver to stand in when backing truck.

sides of the hood and also was used at the front.

A new type of rear axle and spring construction was developed to increase the capacity of the heavy-duty chain-drive Macks. A round axle, six inches in diameter, drilled out to form a tube, was made so as to form a stronger unit without adding excessive weight. To avoid increasing the frame height above normal due to the extra spring leaves, the main springs were slung under the tubular axle. The helper springs were placed on top of the axle, and the combination of tubular axle and underslung spring design became known as the Boulder Dam type. The new Boulder Dam rear end was used on some other AP's and at least one AC produced early in 1932.

Another important feature of the Boulder Dam AP units was a device called a "flexible radius rod," which helped overcome a problem that had caused some chain-drive truck operators a lot of grief. The normal function of the radius rod is to provide a fixed distance between the centers of the driving and driven sprockets, so that the chain will be able to continuously operate with just the right tension and few undue strains from spring flexing. There is usually a provision to adjust the distance in order to take up slack in a worn chain, or adjust for a new chain. However, a serious problem, called "sand lock," would sometimes occur when mud, gravel, or a combination of both got caught between the chain and sprocket. If the mechanism did not crush the material as it passed through, the chain could receive a sudden and terrific increase in tension, and either become jammed on the sprocket or snap at a weak point.

Indications are that Mack engineers had been working on the sand-lock problem prior to the Boulder Dam project, but the combined power and increased carrying capacity of the new AP units focused more attention on the matter. Attached to the forward end of the radius rods, a set of heavy leaf springs was anchored to a frame cross-member by means of the patented Mack rubber shock insulated spring brackets. The new radius rod system was described as "permitting great flexibility and safety, and minimizing strain on all mechanisms."[6]

The bodies used on the huge AP Macks were basically of 14 cubic yards capacity and employed a new type of construction. The sides of the bodies were heavily ribbed and curved inward at the bottom for a smooth super-strong design which could withstand the impact of huge rocks, but afforded few spots for the material to wedge into and resist being dumped out. The welding

Direct side view of the special AP chassis shows heavy fish plating used to reinforce frame side rails. These Super-Duty Macks really began the concept of the modern off-highway truck.

Specially designed welded steel rock bodies, built by the Heil Company, were fitted to most of the AP units at Boulder Dam. Here Heil Company officials observe the operation of one of their units in the spring of 1932.

One aluminum alloy rock body was built by Mack's Los Angeles branch in 1932. Its three-ton saving in weight permitted an equivalent increase in payload. Note riveted construction.

An electric power shovel about to drop a giant boulder into an AP Mack. Workman on left helps clear loose rocks from edge of body, after filling operation, so they will not fall onto access roads and damage tires or cause accidents.

was done on the outside of the bodies, also contributing to their smooth interiors; and no tailgates were employed, which helped to simplify their operation. These rounded rock bodies, called "bathtubs" in the trade, were produced by the Heil Company of Milwaukee, pioneers in welded body construction and the use of under-body hydraulic hoists.

An experimental rock body, made from a special Alcoa aluminum alloy, was constructed by Mack in 1932.[7] Riveted construction was used and a removable subfloor, which rested on two-inch wooden planks, was fitted to the bottom of the body. A weight saving of over 6,000 pounds allowed the capacity to be increased from 14 to 16 yards. The body entered service on August 31, 1932, and was still in excellent shape in November 1933, at the close of the main excavation work.

The bodies were so huge that they blocked the driver's visibility for the necessary backing maneuvers for positioning the vehicle under a shovel, or at the brink of the dump. To overcome this difficulty Mack engineers developed the "Crow's Nest" con-

As the AP on the left takes away about 12 yards of rock, another gets ready to back into position under the power shovel for its share. The bulldozer was used to scrape up spilled material so it could be loaded into another truck.

Concrete work at Boulder Dam progressed rapidly during 1933, with this AP carrying an eight-yard tipple bucket from the mixer to the cableway.

A veteran AP dump chassis later used to carry two 3-1/2 yard concrete mixers, which were electrically driven from power lines just prior to pouring.

Called the "world's largest bus," an AP dump chassis was fitted with a double deck body having eight rows of longitudinal seats for a total capacity of 150. It was used to bring workmen from Boulder City to their jobs during 1933 and 1934.

cept, being a small railed platform mounted on the left-hand side of the driver's compartment, which had auxiliary throttle and brake control.[8] The driver in a standing position facing backward, was able to control the rearward movement of his vehicle entirely beyond the confines of his normal seated position.

A consortium of six contracting companies won the construction contract, with their first major job being the blasting of the huge water diversion tunnels throught the solid canyon walls on both sides of the river. This work was being pushed at top speed by early 1932, with a mixed fleet of 108 trucks including two AP Macks. The greatest number of trucks built by any one manufacturer on the job were five to eight ton capacity, balloon-tired Internationals. These were used in keeping with the

A group of special AC-6 Bulldogs was also used at Boulder Dam. Note new AP-type radiator and balloon tires on both front and rear wheels. It is believed these units were repowered with AP engines soon after their delivery.

Rear view of AC-6 Boulder Dam unit shows under-slung springs, and special axle, apparently forged from a round solid steel billet.

Elevated view of AC-6 rear section shows massive construction. Chassis has inside channel reinforcement for extra strength, air brakes for quicker stopping ability, and flexible radius rod feature to prolong life of drive-chains.

Loading an AC-6 Boulder Dam Bulldog. While the capacity of their bodies was less than the APs, their faster speed gave the AC-6s a quicker turn-around, and, therefore a respectable hauling capability.

prevailing view that the job should be handled with a greater number of units, each carrying lighter loads, but moving a bit faster than extra-heavy-duty rigs hauling more per trip. However, the two Super-Duty Macks soon showed that the solid tires on their rear wheels helped them to handle loads up to 24 tons and, along with their built-in stamina, more than made up for any slight speed advantage shown by the comparatively lighter trucks.

There can be no denying the success of the Super-Duty Mack AP trucks at Boulder Dam. Careful records soon told the correct story of the efficiency of the huge Mack units, and order followed order during the balance of 1932. Some six-cylinder Bulldogs were also ordered, and these differed only slightly in

construction from their AP counterparts. The AC-6 units had slightly small engines, rubber shock insulated spring brackets on the front end, huge dual balloon tires on the rear wheels, and a variation of the rear end found on the AP units. Hood screening, Crow's Nest, and air brakes were standard on both types of Boulder Dam Macks. By early 1933 a fleet of over 20 of the big Macks was engaged in a variety of tough hauling assignments in addition to its intended dumper operation.

The month of July 1933 found the project 18 months ahead of schedule, with nearly all the preliminary excavating and construction work completed shortly after the actual pouring of concrete for the dam proper had begun. The performance of the "Super Bulldogs" which helped to achieve this splendid result

The completed dam as seen from the Colorado River just below the Nevada Powerhouse, on the left, and the Arizona Powerhouse, on the right. The dam was renamed in honor of President Hoover, during whose term the project was started.

A line-up of AP Macks being used on the extensive San Gabriel flood control project in Southern California. Note driver of first truck is standing in the "Crow's Nest."

was commented on by C. P. Bedford, transportation superintendent for the consortium:[9] *"The 'AP' Mack truck has been remarkable in its ability to haul a tremendous load of 14-1/2 to 16 cu. yds. per truck steadily day in and day out with high operating efficiency. As an example, 500 sacks of cement were loaded in to a Mack dump truck. The cement weighed 48,000 lbs. and the truck and dump body weighed 27,000 lbs. This made a gross weight of 75,000 lbs. which was hauled to the Arizona spillway. In one place the truck hauled up 50 feet of 26 percent grade, in which there was a short pitch of 30 percent. Low maintenance cost has been a feature of the Macks in addition to their excellent performance."*

The remarkable achievement by men and machines had as its focal point a public works project which overshadowed all other American building projects, except the Panama Canal, up to that time. The Federal Government bank-rolled the job to the extent of $165 million, but the dollar cost was a very reasonable one when all the benefits were taken into account.

The 115 mile long Lake Mead Reservoir was formed by the dam, which acted as an effective method for controlling floods and providing irrigation water for over one million acres in the southwest. While water supply and control was a prime consideration in constructing the dam, generators were installed at its base to provide low cost hydro-electric power for sections of Arizona, Nevada, and Southern California. It is interesting to note that the dam was renamed Hoover Dam in 1947 in honor of former President Hoover, 1928 - 1932, and that the dam had also been named after him in 1930, but had reverted to its original name, Boulder Dam, with the change in administrations in 1933.

Super-Duty Macks were also used on several other western construction projects during 1933 and 1934. Work began in March 1933 on the San Gabriel flood control project, which involved the construction of a series of rock-fill dams northeast of Los Angeles, California. It was estimated at the time that between 12 and 15 million yards of rock had to be blasted and moved as material for the first dam alone. The main contractor on the job, after observing the AP units at work at Boulder Dam, ordered none but the "Super-Dogs" for all the major rock hauling work.

A fleet of 52 standard Bulldogs was also used on the earth-fill Bouquet Canyon Dam, about 60 miles northwest of Los Angeles. These large projects in the Los Angeles area were part of a huge water management operation created under the

Several six-cylinder Bulldog dumpers were used on the Bonneville Dam project in the Pacific Northwest, starting in the fall of 1934.

The Bonneville Dam project, on the Columbia River, required an extensive dredging operation. This AP Mack is pulling a 16 wheeled Le Tourneau dump trailer, which could carry as much as 61 tons of river muck at one time.

Southern California Metropolitan Water District, with a funding of $250 million.

The Federal Government, under the new Roosevelt Administration, continued to expand its role in the fields of flood control and hydro-electric power through the Public Works Administration. During 1934 several Bulldog six-wheel tractors were employed at the Bonneville Dam project on the Columbia River, about 35 miles west of Portland, Oregon. The balloon-tired six-cylinder Macks were used to haul 35 yard Le Tourneau bottom-dump trailers loaded with as much as 61 tons of river muck at one time.[10]

The AP really proved its worth in the heavy construction field during 1932, and because of its size and carrying capacity deserves to be called America's first off-highway truck. However, the AP was still performing some interestng on-highway services, especially with the introduction of the dual reduction six-wheeler early in 1932. The new balloon-tired six-wheeled AP used the AK bogie and was rated at the same capacity as the AK six-wheeler: eight to 15 tons. However, with its higher horsepower, the AP six-wheeler was well suited for its role as combined freighter and prime mover, with one Philadelphia-based petroleum company using 15 of the units by 1932. A total of 5,200 gallons of gasoline could be hauled by each unit per trip through the use of a large tank body and four-wheeled Mack tank trailer. Unfortunately, a stagnant economy and restrictive motor vehicle weight legislation in many states combined to keep AP truck sales at a very low level throughout the Depression.

Carving A Timeless Memorial

Continuing the marketing strategy of expanding their basic line of modern, six-cylinder trucks, several new B series Macks were introduced during 1931 and 1932. Added to the BJ, BG, BC, and BL models, which had been introduced in that order between 1928 and 1931, were the BF, announced in 1931, and the BM, BX, and BQ, added in 1932. One of the new models was competitive in size and component option to the Bulldog, but all gave potential Mack customers a choice of conventional styling in truck sizes of from one to eight tons nominal capacities.

The new Model BF was offered in the medium-duty capacity of 2-1/2 to four tons, and was powered by the BC engine when introduced in 1931. Only single or dual reduction drive was

A 1931 AP six-wheeler with AK dual reduction four-wheel bogie. Note extra-wide AP radiator, which also became standard on most AC-6 and AK-6 trucks during 1932.

The AP six-wheeler was used in only a few applications. One petroleum company used 15 of these trucks with full-trailers in a tanker operation by 1932.

This 1932 AP tractor has new radiator, large crown fenders, air brakes, and Boulder Dam rear end construction. Built in January of that year.

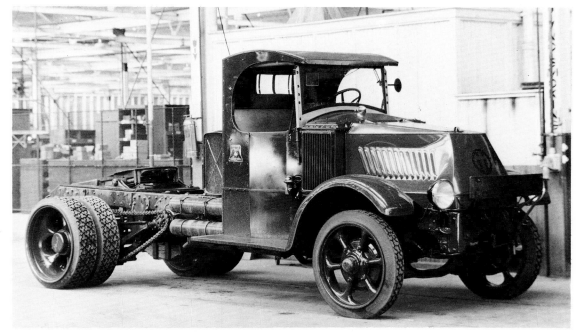

The same 1932 AP tractor pulling a Rogers gooseneck trailer with large block of Georgia marble for the Bronx County Court House. Note front wheels have been converted to balloon tires by the fall of 1932.

141

available on the BF until 1936, when a chain-drive option became available. The BF may have competed for sales with a new six-cylinder version of the traditional AB, which had been introduced in 1930 using the 75 horsepower BG engine. However, the BF was basically too light to have attracted any customers wanting a Bulldog.

The election year of 1932 was almost a disaster from the point of view of the truck manufacturing industry as a whole, with only 228,303 units being sold. This registered as the worst year in the industry since the postwar recession year of 1921, when 148,052 trucks were sold.[11] Mack sales declined accordingly, but three important new models were introduced that year: the BM, BX, and BQ.

Smallest of the new units was the BM, having a nominal capacity of three to five tons and dual reduction drive. Like the BF model, the BM's lighter capacity and lack of chain-drive also precluded its competing with the Bulldog, but it did have the same tonnage rating as the Model AB. The Model BM used the 100 horsepower BC engine, and appealed to customers wanting a more powerful vehicle than the AB.

The next largest model was the BX, rated at four to six tons capacity, and having the new BX engine of 104 brake horsepower. The BX was available with either dual reduction or chain-drive, and soon became a popular dump truck in the medium to heavy-duty class. It effectively replaced the Model BC, which had the same tonnage rating and which was phased out of production by early 1933. As a chain-drive dumper the BX did compete directly with the light and medium-duty AC's, and was really the first modern substitute Mack offered for the traditional 4-Speed Bulldog.

Biggest of the new 1932 B models was the BQ, rated at five to eight tons capacity and having the new BQ engine of 128 brake horsepower. The BQ was described as being a "Long-distance, high-safe-speed schedule-clipper," and was available only with dual reduction.[12] The BQ offered direct competition to the six-cylinder AK of the same five to eight tons capacity, and which had received the BQ engine as a more powerful substitute for its original BK power plant.

After the introduction of the Model BQ, the first of the six-cylinder Mack trucks, the BJ, with a revised capacity of five to eight tons, was phased out. However, due to the increased use of tractor-semi-trailer combinations to meet state axle-load restrictions, the BQ achieved only a limited degree of success as a straight-truck.

Although a complete line of tractor versions of both the AC and AB models had been built since the World War I period, Mack had only offered full-trailers on a regular model basis by 1930. During 1932 a full line of modern semi-trailers in both standard and deep-drop frame designs was announced. Eight basic models, whose capacities ranged from three to 18 tons, were additions to the line of full-trailers introduced earlier. Bulldog tractors, or other Mack models, with Mack semi-trailers became relatively popular combinations with truckers by the mid-1930s.

The styling and construction features of the new 1932 B models reflected the most up-to-date automotive thinking. Set-back front axles gave a better weight distribution, and grouping of chassis lubrication fittings at one point on the frame added to their efficiency. Small doors in their hoods replaced the traditional louvers and added to the neatness of the B models. However, their appearance was far removed from the famous Bulldog they were beginning to replace. This situation must have concerned A. F. Masury, and he must have been pondering ways to remind the public of Mack's Bulldog tradition, with the addition of each new conventional-looking model to the Mack product line.

The opportunity to conceive of a way in which to keep the inspiring image of the famous Bulldog truck in the public's eye, even when viewing one of the more conventional-looking new Macks, came to Masury in an unexpected way. During the spring of 1932, Masury was advised to have a tonsillectomy and was hospitalized for about a week for observation. This was due to the possibility of his catching a bad cold in the changeable weather, which could then cause severe damage to his weakened throat. As a man of action, the prolonged inactivity must have been very trying on his patience and Masury soon came up with an idea to both pass the time and do something constructive for his noble Bulldog's image.

At the time, a large soap company had been sponsoring a nation-wide sculpturing contest, using soap bars instead of clay as the material. Masury summoned one of his aides, John A. Sloan, and requested that he pick up a case of soap and also a small statue he had briefly glimpsed in the window of a Madison Avenue bric-a-brac shop.[13] After receiving the material, Masury busily carved away at the soap bars, settling on a modified cubistic rendering of his beloved canine.

With staunch, squared-off lines, and rampant pose, Masury's Bulldog Mascot had all the no-nonsense, ready-for-work look that symbolized its truck namesake. An application for a design patent was filed with the Patent Office on July 2, 1932, with Design Patent No. 87,931 being granted on October 11, 1932. By early

A conventional looking competitor to the medium and heavy Bulldogs was the Model BX Mack, introduced in 1932. This 1935 unit has the optional chain-drive and a batch body for delivery of building materials.

The chain-drive Model BX became popular with contractors by the late 1930s. This 1937 BX tractor and dump trailer are serving a large New Jersey contractor.

1933 the Bulldog Mascot started to appear as a standard feature atop the radiators of the new Macks as they rolled off the Allentown assembly line, and it was not long before it had become as well-known as the Lincoln Greyhound or the Rolls-Royce Flying Lady!

In addition to his important work as Chief Engineer at Mack, A. F. Masury continued as Chairman of the Ordnance Advisory Committee of the Society of Automotive Engineers, helping to guide the mechanization of the army along sound lines. He was specifically credited with playing an important role in the development, by the Quartermaster Corps, of the first mechanized company to displace the traditional cavalry.

At the first review of the new mechanized force, held at Fort Eustis, Virginia, in 1931, Masury was quoted as saying:[14] *"It is regrettable that the average civilian and politician do not recognize the full importance of the advance made in motor transport since the World War. It handicaps our preparedness and imposes an unnecessary hardship upon our Army personnel who have to struggle along and experiment with designs of the World War period."*

In recognition of his important services to the Army, Masury had been commissioned a Lieutenant-Colonel in the Army through a five year appointment made by President Coolidge, which was renewed by President Roosevelt.[15] His involvement in national defense work was also a partial bridge to a continuing personal interest in the development of lighter-than-air aircraft, which he followed most avidly. The American dirigible program was conducted under the auspices of the Department of the Navy in collaboration with the Goodyear-Zeppelin Corporation, which was actually building the huge craft in America by the late 1920s.

Apparently, Colonel Masury sought eagerly for an invitation to a routine cruise of the 785 foot long U. S. S. Akron, which had recently returned from a round trip journey to the Panama Canal Zone. The Akron was scheduled to leave the Lakehurst Naval Air Station in New Jersey on the evening of Monday, April 3, 1933, and Colonel Masury was driven to Lakehurst by a Mack chauffeur, Norman "Happy" Richmond. On the way down from New York, a local New Jersey motorcycle policeman stopped them for speeding. However, when the judge was informed of the destination of the speeding car, he ordered a motorcycle escort instead of a fine for the offense.[16]

Reaching Lakehurst safely, Masury was one of 76 people on

In this June 1932 photo, the bulldog radiator mascot appears to be straining on a leash in an effort to attack a mighty adversary.

board the U. S. S. Akron when it desengaged from the mooring mast at 7:28 p.m., and quickly rose to its normal cruising altitude of 2,000 feet. Sharing the ride as a passenger with Masury was Rear-Admiral William A. Moffett, Chief of the Navy's Bureau of Aeronautics, and known as "the father" of naval aviation.[17] The craft was under the control of Commander Frank C. McCord, and as it passed Philadelphia, ran into a storm front which had not been indicated by a reading of the afternoon's weather map. As lightning was showing in the sky to the south and west, Commander McCord stated that he planned to keep the Akron in front of the storm, which was traveling in a northeasterly direction.[18]

Weather conditions continued to worsen as the Akron pushed through the swirling clouds and fog banks which obstructed observation of any landmarks. A break appeared in the overcast upon reaching the New York Harbor area, and the craft was turned toward the southeast, but soon caught in the full-force of the storm. The high winds pitched and tossed the Akron to the point it was becoming almost unmanageable. After a few minutes of extreme buffeting the Akron was hit by violent turbulence which literally spun the vertical control wheel out of the elevator-man's desperate grip, dropping the ship about 400 feet. Although the vertical descent was quickly checked, another tremendous gust then caught the ship broadside, causing a rubber control cable to snap.

At this point events were moving very swiftly, with Commander McCord trying with all his skill to stabilize a craft that was quickly losing all means of control. As vital control lines snapped, the Akron began to shudder with the fracturing of its aluminum girders under the tremendous strain inflicted by the storm. The order, "Stand by for a crash," was quickly followed by, "Landing stations," as the craft began its final and uncontrolled descent toward the Atlantic Ocean below.

The U. S. S. Akron split in two as it hit the water off Barnegat Point, New Jersey, shortly after midnight on the morning of April 4th. Only three crewmen of the 76 people on board survived the ordeal, having been rescued by a German freighter which happened on the scene just after the crash. The odds against survival were just too great, as even those people who had managed to get clear of the sinking hulk found their strength ebbing quickly as they struggled to stay afloat in the icy waters.

A massive air-sea search for possible survivors was quickly launched in the early morning hours, but only a few bodies and pieces of scattered wreckage were picked up. Colonel Masury's body was found floating at sea on April 8th, and Commander Mc-Cord's under similar circumstances on the 9th. Rear-Admiral Moffett's body washed ashore near Wildwood, New Jersey, on the 10th. The Akron crash was the worst disaster in aviation history up to that time, and really signaled the end to the Government's

The U. S. Navy Airship Akron, commissioned in 1931, was 785 feet in length, and its eight powerful engines could propel it at nearly 84 mph. Its tragic crash, off the New Jersey coast in April 1933, cost the lives of 73 men including that of Mack's Chief Engineer, A. F. Masury.

By virtue of his rank as Lieutenant-Colonel in the U. S. Army Reserve, A. F. Masury was given a full military funeral aboard the U. S. Coast Guard Cutter Champlain. Colonel Masury's ashes were scattered over the sea near Barnegat Point, New Jersey, on April 13, 1933.

large-scale airship program, as no new dirigible-type craft were finished in the United States after 1933.[19]

In accordance with his expressed wishes, Masury's ashes were taken aboard the U. S. Coast Guard Cutter Champlain, on April 13th, for burial at sea. Over 50 of Masury's relatives, friends, and associates witnessed the simple service on board the cutter, and the scattering of his ashes near the very spot where the U. S. S. Akron had plunged into the sea nine days before. Colonel Alfred Fellows Masury was survived by his mother, Mrs. Evelyn Fellows Masury, and his widow, Mrs. Edna Lanpher Masury.[20]

"A Man For All Seasons"

There can be no question about the high esteem in which Alfred Fellows Masury was held by his friends and associates. Eulogies from various segments of the automotive industry, even from those opposed to some of his views, were praiseworthy of his character and varied contributions. Because of Masury's multi-faceted character, a review of these tributes is necessary in order to gain some idea of the scope of his impact on the industry as well as the people with whom he came in contact.

Without doubt, A. F. Masury's greatest influence was in the development of many special engineering features built into all Mack products, as well as the promotion of their specific qualities, since his elevation to the post of chief engineer during 1914. He supervised an almost constantly growing staff of engineers, and fostered the use of patents to protect Mack's earnest program for developing vehicle components of superior design. Between 1914 and 1934, over 600 patents were assigned to the Mack organization, about 170 of which Masury conceived of either solely or co-invented with members of his staff.[21] From salesman to service manager, and then to chief engineer, Masury had worn all three hats since 1912, and continued to share these responsibilities as part of his concept of building the best product possible.

The loss to his employer, Mack Trucks, Inc., was difficult to comprehend at first, especially since Masury had become such an integral part of so many operating functions. However, Mack President Alfred J. Brosseau tried to indicate the loss in the following sober reflection: *"As one day follows another the Mack organization becomes more impressed with the great loss we have suffered individually and collectively through the untimely death of Alfred Masury. Seldom in the engineering profession do we encounter an individual with traits and abilities as distinctive in character as this man possessed and demonstrated to us on every occasion. His interests were wide and to each he gave careful thought and study. The results will be felt, we believe, for many years to come. All in our organization feel keenly the loss of a close personal friend, and we are grateful for this opportunity of expressing our appreciation of all that he has done for us and our industry."* [22]

Another remembrance of a close business association with Colonel Masury was given by Edward R. Hewitt, whom Masury succeeded in 1914 as chief engineer. Actually, it was E. R. Hewitt who brought Masury to New York in 1907, when he was scarcely 25 years old, to become factory manager of the Hewitt Motor Company. Very much a rugged individual, Hewitt only had praise for Masury's work and character during their many years of collaboration: *"There is no question that much of the success of the engineering problems of the Mack Company has been due to Mr. Masury's work. He was universally liked by all his associates and was extremely popular with the whole automobile trade and all our customers."* [23]

While Alfred Masury never made a claim to being a scientist, he obviously adopted a scientific approach in the experiments he devised, seeking always the practical application for the findings of any new study. The courage shown in Masury's attitude toward design innovations was commented on by Henry M. Crane, Technical Assistant to General Motors Board Chairman, Alfred P. Sloan, and went in part: *"He did not fear to lead if an advance seemed to be possible, but equally he had the courage not to follow a new trend until satisfied that it represented a permanent improvement."* [24]

There were several important unwritten maxims that seemed to be the guiding spirit of Masury's engineering operations at Mack. A design engineer, A. G. Herreshoff, who worked very closely with Masury during the 1916 to 1922 period, spelled these out: *"Always design the simplest and best way you know how, and use the best materials available."* [25]

With the same energy that characterized his work at the Mack organization, Masury pursued his involvement with various engineering societies and trade groups. The generous contribu-

tions of his leadership abilities were most pronounced in the Society of Automotive Engineers, of which he had been a member since 1908. In addition to submitting for publication several original engineering studies on various aspects of motor vehicle construction, Masury took an important part in many forums. All of these activities served the important function of stimulating ideas on ways to overcome problems of design faced by many of the S. A. E. members in their jobs as engineers with various automotive companies, thus helping the industry as a whole.

Along these lines, Masury was very active in the vital role of coordinator of the S. A. E.'s effort to provide up-to-the-minute technical assistance on engineering problems faced by the United States Army in its effort to completely modernize various transport functions. His contributions of time and energy to national defense were praised by Colonel C. M. Wesson of the Ordnance Department in the following statement: *"I have been closely associated with Colonel Masury for the past three years, during which time he was Chairman of the Ordnance Advisory Committee of the Society of Automotive Engineers. From my association with him I formed for him the highest regard, both as an engineer and as a man.* [26]

It seems hard to conceive of a person, who put so much energy into his official duties and related collateral activities, having any inclination to participate in sports or hobbies in spare moments. However, A. F. Masury was basically a lover of life who greeted involvement in all its phases, and outdoor sports were one of his early interests. His life-long friend and associate, John F. Winchester, remembered how he had first met Alfred Masury at a local high school track meet, observing his successful efforts to score points in the shot-put contest for his team. [27]

Although Masury kept up his basic interest in all kinds of sports, attending track meets as well as golf, boxing and racing events, he apparently did not participate much physically, and tended to gain weight in later years. This situation may have come about by his chief recreation of boating.

Colonel Masury's yacht served as a personal forum where he could expound his ideas on a variety of subjects to his many guests. His whole background of working a minimum of 10 hours a day and very often putting in 14-hour days when overtime was necessary, combined with his basic enthusiasm to find well-developed solutions to every problem that confronted him. Con-

"Mack is the Truckman's Truck," and it could be said that it was A.F. Masury's truck, too. It was his guiding light that had helped so much in building Mack and making it the "Truckman's Truck." (Motor Truck News, April, 1932)

sidering this background in his training and work habits, it was only natural that these opinions might be delivered in a forceful way at times.

In summation, it should be said that Alfred Fellows Masury brought a sense of purpose to any task he undertook. This attitude demanded his best performance, and also inspired his associates to give their best to any project he was directing. His dedication to hard work did not over-shadow a strong feeling for humanity, for he was never known to ignore anyone believing that everyone should be heard regardless of his station in life. As all the eulogies indicate, Colonel Masury was an outstanding character whose many efforts affected more than the course of automotive design. His willingness to give good council and devotion to principle surely rank him as one of those rare individuals we could call, "A man for all seasons."

The Narrow Pneumatic Bulldog

During 1933 the 4-Speed Bulldog Mack began to enter its final phase of production, with several major component changes being readied for a new and final version to be introduced in 1934. The demand for new Macks of the size and service capabilities of the Models AC, AK, and AP had fallen dramatically due to the Depression, with production of these models dropping to a combined total of about 60 units during 1933. Few, if any, of these trucks were built for stock, as all heavy-duty models became part of the "Custom Line" by the mid-1930s, and orders for such units had to be channeled to a special equipment engineer to insure the matching of the vehicle's specifications to its intended duties. However, the adaptability of the basic Bulldog chassis to the changing economic conditions and technical advances that were influencing truck design enabled the Model AC Mack to satisfy a small, but steady, demand up to 1938, its final year of production.

The basic need for the third version of the Bulldog was to enable it to use dual pneumatic tires and still keep within the 96 inch overall width limit, which most states stipulated as a requirement for any motor vehicle operated on the public roads. Narrowing the overall width of the chain-drive six-wheel AC and AP had already been accomplished by 1931, with the elimination of the traditional jackshaft brakes, as well as by some changes in spring bracket design. Changes made in the chain-drive six-

This handsome AC-6 Bulldog tractor was completed in the fall of 1932. Note use of improved AP radiator, and guard for drive-chain in front of quarter rear fender.

Rear view of new six-cylinder Bulldog tractor reveals new narrow tubular axle, and springs set directly under the frame rails. This new narrow rear end design reduced the overall width of the Bulldog.

wheelers did not involve the basic I-beam axle design, but the new concept for the four-wheeled AC included a different type of axle and spring placement to achieve a reduction of overall width without reducing the frame width from its 37-1/2 inches.

A lack of uniformity in the laws governing overall width limits among the various states complicated the truck builder's task of compliance. Some states permitted up to 108 inches across the rear tires for conversions from solids, while others simply allowed a 102 inch width to encourage the purchase of balloon-tired equipment. However, some states having the 96 inch requirement enforced a measurement taken at the bulge of the tire where it rested on the road, with the result that the effective truck width was cut by almost two inches.[28] With the trend to balloon tires on larger and larger trucks, the overall width problem really tested the ingenuity of the heavy-duty truck designers, especially those working on chain-drive models.

A very neat looking balloon-tired AC-6 tractor, with coupe cab, was completed during the fall of 1932. The tractor's six-cylinder engine was cooled by the larger AP-type radiator, which became a standard component on the AC-6 and AK-6 during 1933.

Prototype AC-4 dumper chassis with new narrow tubular axle, completed early in 1932. Note elimination of jackshaft brakes.

Worm's eye view of new dumper chassis shows Boulder Dam rear end setup with under-slung main springs. Note also new steel radius rod design.

The rear axle was of the improved tubular-type which had proven so successful on the new AP Boulder Dam units. The rear springs were positioned directly under the frame rails, instead of being placed in the usual outboard mounting. With the elimination of the jackshaft brakes, the driving sprockets were mounted closer to the frame side rails, thus providing a closer clearance for the dual tires and reducing the normal overall rear width.

Other changes noted on the new AC tractor included air brakes, and a disc-type emergency brake which was mounted behind the transmission. The placement of the disc brake in back of the transmission, instead of on the propeller shaft in front of it, was a necessary feature to avoid a failure in braking action in case the gears were placed in neutral.

Another prototype AC unit having the new tubular, narrow axle concept, was completed early in 1932. However, this four-cylinder Bulldog was designed for extra-heavy service, as it had solid tires, and the springs were slung under the axles as well as being positioned directly under the frame side rails. While the underslung spring construction with helper springs on top of the axles, was apparently developed for the Boulder Dam AP's, it promised greater hauling capacity for other chain-drive Mack models as well.

Top view of chassis shows leaf spring setup for flexible radius rod device, located just behind jackshaft housing.

Test truck of the new CH and CJ cab-over-engine models was completed in the summer of 1933. Note slight Bulldog hood shape in the radator shell, which was not carried through in the final design of the production units.

The year 1933 also marked the rebirth of the cab-over-engine truck, in a modernized version, in order to meet legal length restrictions with long bodies, or when used as a tractor to pull semi-trailers.[29] The c. o. e. design, which had been popular in the United States just prior to the World War I period, also achieved a desirable 1/3 - 2/3 distribution of weight on the front and rear axles. This had the result of maximizing the loading space in relation to the vehicle's overall length, and also helped to utilize more fully the various state legal limitations on axle loadings. The cab-over-engine truck again won recognition as a logical unit for use in urban delivery service, due in part to its greater maneuverability.

A Mack prototype c. o. e. model completed in mid-1933, had a radiator shell having the general shape of the Bulldog hood when faced head-on. The 1933 prototype most likely evolved from the AFM experimental unit that had been completed late in 1930. However, the CH and CJ production models, introduced late in 1933, had exposed radiators of regular design and only the Bulldog mascot was left to remind one of its original background. The new Mack c. o. e. models were called Traffic Types, and proved to be well suited to heavy urban delivery service.

In fact, the CJ Mack of 3-1/2 to six tons capacity really replaced the Bulldog in quite a few of its more general hauling tasks. Some of the more traditional uses for the Model AC, such as coal and petroleum delivery, newsprint trucking, pier work, asphalt distribution for highway improvement, and even general haulage needs of circuses, gradually gave way in many cases to the Model CJ Mack. Although the CJ did not have the chain-drive feature, its dual reduction drive and its use of the same major components as the Model BX, fitted it as a worthy replacement for the Bulldog during the mid to late 1930s.

The year 1933 was topped-off with the repeal of prohibition, which resulted in the reopening of many breweries across the country and their consequent need for many types of trucks. Many Bulldog Macks had been sold to the brewing industry prior to the Volstead Act of 1919 and the shut-down of nearly all breweries, but few, if any, new Model AC's entered this service again. However, the Model AK Mack proved very attractive to several New York area brewers, and a few large fleets of AK's entered this service between 1933 and 1936. There was even a special low-bed AK model that was adapted to the delivery of beer in kegs. These were all shaft-drive units, as the chain-drive AK versions had been phased out during 1932.

Final phase out of the 4-Speed Bulldog, which had been built since 1922 with only minor changes, took place during 1934. About 700 of the medium-duty AC Macks were built between 1930 and 1934, and over 300 of the light-duty units had been produced during the same period. A little under 200 units of the heaviest type were built in the same time frame. Having its main sales tied to the contracting and building supply fields, Bulldog production had suffered along with the hard-hit construction industry since the start of the Depression.

A group of ten new AK-4 brewery trucks parade on New York's fashionable 57th Street in the spring of 1935.

The complete repeal of Prohibition early in 1933 brought a flood of orders to the truck manufacturers. Mack sold a large group of AK-4s to New York brewers, such as this 1936 delivery unit.

There was even a special drop-frame AK-4 designed for the brewery trade, which provided a lower body height for easier loading and unloading of the heavy kegs.

Unloading the kegs on the traditional rope mat cushion at the Crossroads of the World.

Drop-frame Model AK-4 built in 1932 for use with special rotary-type sanitation body. Note frame has been built-up from several sections, unlike the later brewery truck chassis.

A mid-1920s Bulldog that was rebuilt with an attachment axle
and Budd steel disc wheels. Oil field hoist was supplied by
Hopper Machine Works of Bakersfield, California, about 1930.

One of the last four-speed Bulldog dumpers to be built. This
1934 unit has high pressure pneumatics with special lug-type
tread developed for off-highway use.

The final large groups of 4-Speeders for city trucking service
went to a newsprint delivery firm in New York City during 1934.
Note long wheelbase and extreme length of body.

The growth of the fuel oil business in the early 1930s prompted the rebuilding of this circa 1928 Model AC-4 to a six-wheel tanker in the summer of 1933. The Heil tank body had a capacity of 3,000 gallons.

A stock Bulldog of the New "Narrow Pneumatic" type, which went into production during the spring of 1934. Note use of shock insulated front spring brackets.

Another factor which restricted the sale of new Model AC Macks was the surplus units that were available in the used truck market. Many of these, some dating as far back as the World War I period, were still in very serviceable condition and found a market with smaller firms and individuals unable to afford a new model. Many a used chassis found its way into crane-carrier service, starting about this time. Others were overhauled and rebuilt for strip-mining service in Pennsylvania, after serving as city delivery trucks for many years. Second and third "lives" for Bulldogs, often in heavier service than their first, were proof of the outstanding quality built into these trucks.

The year 1934 was a very opportune one for the introduction of the Narrow Pneumatic version of the Bulldog, with a revival of the economy giving confidence to the private sector of the construction industry. Total truck sales reached 576,205 units in 1934,[30] the best year since 1929 for the truck industry, and enabled Mack to show a modest profit of $17 thousand on total sales of $18.3 million.[31] Production of Mack AC, AK, and AP models reached over 200 units, about the same as were built in 1932.

Both the AC-4 and AC-6 were now offered in a nominal capacity of seven to nine tons with the same basic tubular axle and spring suspension. The four-cylinder Bulldog continued to use its standard Model AC engine, and the AC-6 retained the BQ engine it had acquired in 1932. Cooling systems were basically the same on both models, except that the AC-6 used the larger AP radiator. Vacuum assisted four-wheel mechanical brakes were standard equipment, with air brakes available as an option. New tubular and channel type cross-members gave the frame added strength, and a separate bracket was added for the radius rod, which had previously been attached to the jackshaft support bracket. The letters L, M, and H were dropped in the chassis number coding, and the letter N was substituted.

Being considered a slow-speed lugger, geared mainly for crowded city streets and climbing out of deep excavations in first gear, the new AC-4 had solid tires as standard equipment when first introduced. However, the larger crown-type fenders were standard equipment and presented an odd sight on the few Nar-

Right-hand side view of 1934 Narrow Pneumatic Bulldog shows use of four-wheel brakes and tie-rod placement behind front axle.

Interior view of Narrow Pneumatic cab shows some added dashboard details, but still in keeping with the Bulldog's no-frills rugged construction. The flexible rubber steering wheel was not used on the new AC series since most units came equipped with balloon tires.

Top view of Narrow Pneumatic chassis shows improved construction features, such as twin vacuum booster brake cylinders, and parking brake located under special cross-member just behind jackshaft housing.

Side view of 1934 AC-4 Bulldog with Boulder Dam rear end. Solid tires and four-cylinder engines restricted their speed to such an extent that they lost any advantage of their extra carrying capacity.

Direct rear view of AC-4 "Boulder Dam" chassis shows main springs slung under the heavy tubular rear axle. Also, helper springs were on top, which was just the opposite to normal N.P. rear spring design.

Most Narrow Pneumatic Bulldogs had helper springs under their tubular rear axles. This 1934 N.P. chassis has only the main springs installed in their new position, directly under the frame rails.

row Pneumatics that were actually sold with solid tires on all four wheels. Some customers did specify a combination of balloon tires on the front wheels and solids on the rear of their new Bulldogs. The AC-6 being more powerful and considerably faster had balloon tires as standard equipment. Demand for the new Bulldogs was especially strong among contractors and building supply companies, although some haulers of bulk commodities, such as coal, also purchased the new type Model AC.

The Boulder Dam rear axle and underslung spring suspension continued to be the basis for the higher capacity off-highway Bulldogs that were built in both four and six-cylinder models. Apparently the demand for Mack off-highway trucks slackened in the construction industry, but boomed in the mining industry. New types of quarry bodies, based on the bathtub-type units built

for Boulder Dam, were soon being supplied for AC-4, AC-6, and AP units. The extra capacity of the Boulder Dam rear end was utilized by a few New York building supply firms which ordered Bulldogs for use with huge batch-type sand and gravel bodies. A nominal capacity of 10 to 15 tons was logical for these special AC-4 and AC-6 Macks.

By the end of 1934, AC-6 off-highway units had been redesigned with conventional front spring brackets and Boulder Dam rear ends. Extremely tough lug-type tires became available about this time, and the solid tire virtually disappeared from off-highway service. Air brakes became a popular option on the huge off-highway Bulldogs, which most likely had a capacity in the 15 to 20 ton range. The AC-6 units sold for urban dumper service also had modified front spring suspension construction by 1935. Also during this year, most Bulldog cabs were modified with a rounded corner by their pull-up or hinged-type doors.

The most exciting development for the motor truck industry during the 1930s was the perfection of the automotive-type diesel engine. The Cummins Engine Company of Columbus, Indiana, which had been building small industrial-type diesels since the early 1920s, succeeded in demonstrating the practicality of one of their engines for use in heavy-duty trucks during 1931 and 1932. With the basic thermal efficiency of the diesel being almost double that of most gasoline engines, and with the still untaxed diesel fuel for less than half the price of gasoline, the slogan, "Twice as far for half as much," had much credence to it. However, the higher initial cost of the engine did tend to limit sales for the first five or six years, with most installations being the repowering of older trucks by fleet owners interested in seeing if the diesel was suitable for their type of service.

During 1935 and 1936 several Bulldog Macks were repowered with Cummins four-cylinder diesels, with the happy

The great economic advantage of diesel power as applied to trucks created a demand for engine conversions during the 1930s. Here a Cummins diesel powered AK-6 is shown hauling a huge prefabricated ship part, weighing 35 tons, near the main Mack Allentown plants during World War II.

result that no modifications had to be made in the drive systems of the trucks, since the new engine matched the original torque and horsepower characteristics. The success of two diesel engines prompted one contractor, operating in Brooklyn, New York, to order 18 more, and then a fleet of AC-4 chassis to match them, early in 1937.[32] The actual installation of the Cummins HB-4 engines was handled in New York City, with certain modifications to the engine compartments being made at Allentown. Steering gear assemblies had to be shifted so as to clear the large single-disc fuel pumps, and special support brackets were installed with the engines. The following year, a building supply firm in Flushing, New York, ordered 11 new AC-6 dumpers with HB-6 Cummins engines. This was handled as a factory installation, with the letter D appearing as a suffix at the end of the chassis number on each truck.

Unfortunately for the Model AC, and the other Bulldog-like Macks, the end was in sight for their production by 1936. The first to be phased out was the Model AK, which had a total production of 34 units in 1936, its final year. Competition from the new dual reduction B model Macks, as well as the obsolescence factor in the truck's styling, contributed to falling customer interest. The AP model also suffered from continuing low production, with only 12 being produced in 1935 and 14 in 1936. Production records also indicate that 1936 was the last year for the venerable AB Mack, with only 28 being built.

A new series of chain-drive super-duty Macks was in the final stages of design during 1936, with the first of the models, the FC, being completed by November of that year. The Model FC was comparable in hauling capacity to the Model AP, but had a frontal placement of the radiator and various refinements in the following years, such as new axles and multi-speed transmissions. Several four and six-wheel FC Macks were built for the mining industry during 1937, with no production of AP units being recorded. The year 1938 saw the last four AP Macks roll off the Allentown assembly line, marking the tenth anniversary of the building of the first Super-Duty prototype unit in 1928.

Only Bulldogs to have factory installed diesels were a group of eleven AC-6s delivered to a New York City building supply firm in 1938. Note disappearance of Bulldog nameplate from side of cab, which coincided with the name change of the International Motor Co. to Mack Manufacturing Corp.

An HB-6 Cummins diesel engine, the type of engine installed in the 1938 AC-6 diesel Bulldogs. This particular engine has not been modified for use with the Bulldog's Type V cooling system.

The last AK Macks were produced in 1936 in both four and six-cylinder versions. This AK-6, with telescoping hoist, was delivered in June 1936.

A new chain-drive F-Series was developed by Mack between 1936 and 1939 to replace the famous Bulldog. This Model FCSW unit was completed in September 1937.

Model AP with chain-drive bogie was built in late 1935 for a mining company. The capacity of this Super-Duty Mack must have exceeded 20 tons.

A 1936 AP dumper with Easton bathtub body. Except for their larger engines, most AP four-wheeled off-highway trucks were similar in basic design to AC-6 off-highway units.

New Mack, Jr. 1936 Model 20MB poses alongside contemporary AC-6, for a "Mutt and Jeff" photo. The second Mack, Jr. line was only built during 1936 and 1937.

Big changes in the light and medium-duty product line, as well as the Mack organization, were also under way during 1936. In an effort to expand basic product sales in order to help cover branch and dealer over-head costs, a line of streamlined trucks, in capacities of 1/2 to 3 tons, was offered during 1936 and 1937. This new line was called the Mack, Jr. and was built by the Reo Motor Car Company.[33] Also, the first of a completely new Mack "E" series, the Model EH, was introduced in 1936, being greatly expanded by the end of 1938 to replace the Mack, Jr. line in most capacities. One of the new E models, the ER, was offered with chain-drive, thus providing a vehicle in the capacity of the discontinued Model AB. The ER was basically an EH with an AB chain-drive rear end.

The new product lines and general revival of business resulted in a net profit of $1.4 million on sales of $30.8 million in 1936.[34] Unfortunately, the services of some of the senior officials who had seen the Mack organization safely through the worst days of the Depression were suddenly lost. Mack President since 1917, Alfred J. Brosseau, died in September 1936, and his successor, Charles Hayden, of the investment banking house of Hayden, Stone & Company, died suddenly in January 1937. Shortly after the passing of Hayden, Emil C. Fink, long-time Mack

production manager, became president. Also at this time, the name of the main producing arm of the Mack organization, the International Motor Company, was changed to Mack Manufacturing Corporation. Mack Trucks, Inc., continued as before in the role of parent company.

In its final years of production, the Bulldog truck was built in the gross vehicle weight range of 35,000 to 50,000 pounds, with the proper modifications to suspensions and tire sizes to meet the required capacity. When working out details for the new F series, it was determined that each model would cover a 5,000 g. v. w. range starting at 35,000 g. v. w. During the spring of 1938, the following F models, with their respective maximum g. v. w.'s, went into production: FG, 35,000; FH, 40,000; FJ, 45,000; and FK, 50,000.

The basic characteristic of the F models, besides their chain-drive, was the use of a narrower frame, and unit power plant and transmission in conformity with the concept in effect since the introduction of the modern six-cylinder models. Another feature of most of the new models was a prominently set-back front axle for better weight distribution.

During the last two years of Bulldog production, the off-highway units went to mining operations in the east and midwest, while regular street vehicles found their strongest market in the New York City construction industry. A building boom had developed in the metropolitan area by 1937, with the building of parkways, tunnels, and apartment projects requiring the removal as well as delivery of huge amounts of materials. Building of the New York World's Fair and LaGuardia Airport were well under way when Model AC production was phased out in the spring of 1938. A total of 74 AC-4 and AC-6 units were produced in 1937 and 21 in 1938.

The demise of the Bulldog Mack, as an active production model, marked more than the end of one era. Model AC Macks had been produced steadily since 1916 and had served the country well during the national emergency of World War I. The Roaring Twenties saw the Bulldog become the country's premier heavy-duty truck, with its snub-nosed hood and chain-drive providing for an unusually high level of public recognition.

Finally, the Great Depression of the 1930s witnessed the Bulldog's participation in the various Federal and privately sponsored construction projects which helped to lift the nation out of a period of economic stagnation. Many Bulldogs continued to provide an economic return to their owners long after other heavy-duty trucks of a similar age were worn out, and they were not uncommon sights in several big cities up to the 1960s. The expression, "Built like a Mack truck," surely had its origins in the public recognition of an outstanding truck that will live on in the annals of automotive history as one of the really famous vehicles of all-time!

- Fini -

A six-cylinder Bulldog leads a parade of B and F series chain-drive Mack dumpers across a bridge in Flushing Bay, New York. Construction project was the 1938 enlargement of the North Beach Airport, later renamed LaGuardia Airport after New York City's famous mayor.

The Bulldog Tradition — Corporate Symbol And Product Mascot

There is certainly no more easily identifiable trademark in the world of commerce than Mack's Bulldog symbol. Although spawned by the appearance of the Model AC Mack truck during the hectic days of World War I, the outstanding performance of the AC Mack soon proved its right to the same name as one of the canine kingdom's most determined and fearless breeds. The development and various uses of the bulldog as the Mack corporate symbol and radiator mascot is one of the outstanding success stories of the automotive industry.

The comment by members of an English purchasing delegation inspecting Model AC Macks in the spring of 1917, that "their pugnacious front and resolute lines suggest the tenacious quality of the British bulldog," appears to be the starting point for a long lasting alliance: the bulldog and Mack trucks! By the summer of 1917 Mack advertisements featuring the Model AC now identified it as the "Bull Dog," usually using two separate words. The use of two words may have been due to the U. S. trademark laws which generally restrict the freedom to copyright words of a generic nature.

Finally, in the summer of 1920, the picture of a bulldog started to appear in Mack advertisements. However, the Mack Bulldog was not shown in a relaxed position. On the contrary, it was shown with a torn book entitled *Hauling Costs*, in its mouth, and a broken restraining muzzle, labeled *Competition*, laying at its feet. This white coated bulldog had a determined look in its eye, and had all the earmarks of a natural winner.

By late 1921, the vignette of the "Bull Dog" tearing up *Hauling Costs* was incorporated into a new nameplate that was affixed to both sides of AB and AC Mack cabs. The new nameplate was in the shape of the Model AC hood when viewed head-on, and became a traditional part of the Bulldog Mack until late 1936.

During the mid-1920s radiator temperature indicators, called Motometers, became popular as an accessory for placing on top

Putting finishing touches to exit of west-bound section of Lincoln tunnel, between New York and New Jersey. A pre-1930 Bulldog crane truck is removing timber scaffolding late in 1937

By 1921 a large nameplate was devised which incorporated the bulldog tearing up hauling cost scene. The nameplate was in the shape of the Bulldog Mack's hood when viewed head-on, and was used on all Model AC cabs up to the end of 1936.

During 1920 Mack Truck advertisements started to carry a scene showing a bulldog using its teeth to tear up a book entitled, "Hauling Costs." A muzzle labeled, "Competition," lies at his feet.

Even the decal used by Mack's Long Island City custom body building shop was based upon a front view of the Bulldog's hood.

This 3/4-side view of the Bulldog Radiator Mascot was taken in June 1932, just a few months after its design by A. F. Masury.

A rear-side view of the mascot reveals A.F. Masury's initials cast into the canine's left rear foot.

The mascot lost his original pedestal atop some Mack radiator caps when the streamlined E series trucks, with concealed radiators, were introduced in 1938. However, the problem was solved by the design of a special moulding to provide a perch for the cast-canine.

Close-up of radiator tank on 1936 Model BM, six-cylinder truck, shows normal installation of mascot and new enameled oval Mack nameplate.

of the normally plain automotive radiator cap. However, by the late 1920s various kinds of small metal statury started to replace the Motometers on certain makes of trucks and cars, with the objects having, in many cases, some significance as a company or product symbol. These radiator ornaments were soon referred to as "mascots," as they were often in the shape of an animal or human being.

As related in Chapter IV, Mack's Chief Engineer, Alfred F. Masury, received a patent on the Bulldog radiator mascot that he designed during 1932. It was this novel canine radiator mascot that soon caught the public's eye and so positively linked the bulldog with the Mack truck. The Bulldog's angular lines and rampant stance at the front of every conventional Mack truck transmitted the fabulous reputation of the Model AC: Ready, Willing and Able to perform its assigned duties!

Starting with the Model EH introduced in 1936, all subsequent E series Mack trucks had their radiator caps concealed under a modern radiator grill and sheet metal shell. Since the

The prewar rounded mascot as he looked on a special pedestal needed to support all of his four feet. Wisely, it was never substituted in its full three-dimensional version for A. F. M.'s more rugged-looking canine.

This tough-looking canine, developed in 1945, seems to be a compromise between A. F. M.'s stylized bulldog and the rounded 1941 version. It apparently never went beyond the design stage.

The so-called "corporate canine" most likely inspired this rounded version of the mascot, produced in 1941. A bas-relief adaptation of this design was later used as a hood mascot on many Mack truck models.

Bulldog mascot could not be attached to the radiator caps on these models, it was placed atop a neat chromed center moulding over the top of the grill just in front of the engine hood.

In an apparent effort to create a Bulldog mascot more in the likeness of the "corporate canine," a new rounded version was designed by the fall of 1941. Since it rested on all four feet, a prototype pedestal was created to display the mascot properly at the front of the E or new L series trucks. This experimental design project was no doubt shelved by the American involvement in World War II a couple of months later. However, a side view, or silhouette, of the rounded Bulldog mascot was used on the sides of the hoods on the A series Mack trucks introduced in 1950. It continued in use in the same position on the subsequent B series trucks.

Another attempt to design a new Bulldog mascot was tried late in 1945, with the concept an apparent compromise between the rounded corporate canine and the angular mascot. The new metal mascot rested on all four feet and had highly modified squared-off lines, mainly in its leg areas. The new postwar mascot, although cleverly styled, still did not convey the same message produced by a quick look at Masury's rampant canine, and was not adopted.

The only major change to the Corporate Bulldog, since its inception in 1920, occurred in 1965 when its white coat was changed to a brindle color in a fine rendering by the painter, Joseph Csatari. This change was part of a corporate advertising strategy instituted by the then new President, Zenon C. R. Hansen, to capitalize on the public awareness of the Mack Bulldog. Full-color prints of the new life-like Bulldog symbol were

The Corporate Bulldog sign as erected on the front fascia of Mack's World Headquarters building in Allentown. It is translucent and fully illuminated at night.

made up for Mack offices, and many new Bulldog emblazoned novelties were developed with the aid of Keith Smykal Associates. The most novel use of the corporate symbol, no doubt, is on the lapel pins which visitors to Mack's Allentown facilities are invited to wear by one of their charming receptionists.

Not only is Allentown the place to see the most miniature Mack Bulldogs, it is also the place to see what has been called

Preserved early Mack sightseeing bus serves as the historic prop for this "Beauty and the Beast" scene.

B'JEEZ, ME BRAKES AINT WOIKEN!

World-famous industrial artist, Peter Helck, did this imaginative scene of a Bulldog stake truck crashing into a World War II Nazi tank while rushing war supplies to the North-African front.

A 1940 Model EHU Traffic-Type Mack was the chassis on which this replica Bulldog van was built. The Baltimore mover, a long time Bulldog Mack user, had two such units in use up to the late 1950s.

1940 DeLuxe Model

the world's largest. With the decision in 1965 to construct a large corporate headquarters at Allentown, plans for the structure soon followed as did discussions regarding a suitable sign for the building's facade. In talks with representatives of the Federal Sign and Signal Corporation, the decision was finally reached that a huge fiberglass Corporate Bulldog could, by itself, convey the ownership of the building.

During the summer of 1969, the 17 x 20 foot hand-moulded translucent image was fabricated in four sections at Federal Sign's Blue Island, Illinois, plant, and shipped to Allentown. By the use of concealed stainless steel supporting pegs, the huge Corporate Bulldog has presented the pleasing aesthetic effect of "floating" on the front of the headquarters building. And, with the aid of back-lighting, this floating effect is heightened at night, with the Bulldog not only silhouetted but also displaying its brindle color in a warm glow coming through the fiberglass material.

It has certainly been a successful marriage between that noble canine, the bulldog, and the Mack organization, since that casual remark in 1917 brought them both together.

Mock-up of proposed postwar Model EE truck shows Bulldog influence in grill design. Note bulldog mascot peaking out of semi-circular dog house.

Design of frontal area of this proposed postwar M-8 truck model showed strong influence of Bulldog hood design.

Mack AC Epilogue — The Indestructable Bulldog

Bulldogs with Long Service Records

The history of the mighty Bulldog Mack does not, by any means, end with the completion of the last AC-6 units by the Allentown plant in December of 1938. Since that time the actual service life of the average Model AC seemed to be almost unlimited, as many owners continued to use their Bulldogs for decades after the normal retirement point for similar types of vehicles. A very strong market for used Bulldogs was evidenced in some areas up to the 1950s, with actual outright scrapping still a rarity. Such owner loyalty to a specific truck model can only be explained by the Bulldog's tremendous reliability, proving there could not have been a more apt nickname used to describe this ageless wonder of the motor vehicle industry.

Old solid-tired Bulldog Macks were a common sight in the New York City area for many years after World War II. The biggest users at that time were general haulage concerns which trucked foreign trade commodities to and from the many piers and warehouses in the port area. One of the largest truckers in this field used nothing but second-hand Bulldogs, up to the mid-1950s, which dated from the mid-1920s. Other venerable AC Macks in the area were used to transport coal, building materials, and heavy machinery. One of the very last AC's licensed for regular street work was operated by a Brooklyn, New York, rigger up to the mid-1970s, and then retired for preservation.

The City of Baltimore, Maryland, also had a large group of Bulldog Macks in an important public service long after World War II. These had been used by the Fire Department in such capacities as tractors for aerial ladders, high-pressure pumpers, and for miscellaneous support services. Many of the B. F. D. Bulldogs were 3-Speeders from the World War I period that had been modernized over the years with balloon tires, even receiving streamlined sheet metal in a few cases.

Some trucking companies used Bulldogs as terminal tractors to shift semi-trailers to and from loading docks or parking areas. Such units were usually second-hand, or may have even

been straight jobs that were cut down to serve as short wheelbased tractors. A 1928 Bulldog tractor was in almost daily use in the yard of a large Detroit area dairy up to the mid-1970s, although it did have a replacement engine.

Other Bulldogs have served as unlicensed yard trucks for several large scrap metal and industrial companies around the country. A Bulldog at the Long Island, New York, plant of a large copper refining company was still in daily use up to the spring of 1978, having delivered a half-century of service since being delivered new to its first owners, a Brooklyn lumber yard, in May 1928.

Big cities have not been the only stamping ground for vintage Bulldogs, as the oil fields of Southern California can testify. Mack AC's were very popular in the California petroleum industry by the early 1920s, serving a wide variety of functions from tankers to oil well servicing units. A few 3-Speeders built prior to 1922, as well as 4-Speeders from the mid and late-1920s, have been used as winch trucks up to the mid-1970s. And a few of

A 1928 5-1/2 ton Bulldog which realized its 50th anniversary of work in the New York City area on May 4, 1978. It is still powered by a Mack AC engine, although the cab has been rebuilt.

Circa 1929 Bulldog being used as a terminal tractor by an over-the-road trucking company at the end of World War II. The LFT Mack tractor on the left is a brand new unit delivered under a governmental allocation system regarding essential use.

these vehicles are believed to be still doing an occasional day's work in 1979, although the rest are being acquired by collectors.

There have even been reports in the early and mid-1970s of Bulldog Macks still operating in Denmark, Puerto Rico, and Cuba. The average age of these vehicles must be at least 50 years, and certainly prove the traditional Mack slogan: "Performance Counts."

Some Unusual Rebuilt Units

The adaptability of Bulldogs to many extreme requirements of service, even as they reached a normal retirement age, was matched only by the ingenuity of the mechanics who attempted some highly unusual transformations. These changes were apart from, and really above and beyond, the more common use of replacement engines such as Cummins diesel; or the conversion to balloon tires and switch to faster drive chain ratios.

The main radical changes to Bulldogs involved the replacement of the standard AC engine and cooling system. Various kinds of faster gasoline engines were substituted and a new radiator installed in front. The original Bulldog hood had to be discarded in many cases and a new one devised by a sheet metal shop. To provide additional cooling for some of the 3-Speeders operating on the West Coast, an hexagonally-shaped replacement radiator was installed, which circled the fan, and an outer radiator also added for a greater combined cooling capacity.

Bulldog Macks have even undergone some extreme structural changes in their rebuilding into crane carriers. At least one truck equipment company took a group of Bulldogs completely apart, substituting large structural steel I-beams for the original heat-treated pressed-steel frame members. Apparently all, or nearly all, of the original components were then reinstalled in the new chassis frame. This unusual transformation provided an extremely stiff frame and most likely a capacity double the original.

There were many other Bulldog crane carrier conversions, but most of these retained the original frames, although additional fish-plating was added to strengthen them. Some Bulldog crane trucks were still in use in various parts of the country up to the mid-1970s, if not later.

Some unusual six-wheel conversions took place on the West Coast, mostly in California. Due to local motor vehicle laws restricting axle loads and the distance between the axles, the

A large New Jersey brewery rebuilt a fleet of Bulldogs, replacing engines and cooling systems with newer conventional components. Note unusual hood design and wooden-spoked front wheels.

Rebuilt 1928 Model AK Mack with GMC Model 400 six-cylinder engine. Note new lower hood and inverted AK bumper to provide more air for frontal placement of Yellow Coach radiator.

conversion of four-wheeled trucks to six-wheelers became a big field for truck equipment firms in this area and sometimes took on extreme forms. One 1921 3-Speed Bulldog has been found which has an attachment third-axle mounted several feet ahead

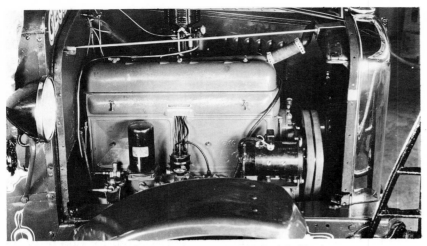

Close-up of engine installation on rebuilt 1928 AK Mack showing snug fit of new engine. Rebuilding took place in 1933, and was done for a Detroit-area cartage company.

This World War I Bulldog had seen many years of service in France when this picture was taken in 1945. The large drum at the side of cab was used to heat wood chips which produced a distilate-type gas that fueled the engine. This energy producing device was needed due to an almost complete disruption of gasoline supplies by the end of World War II.

of the rear axle, with wheels that steer with the front wheels. The linkage and parts for controlling the steering of the attachment wheels are all locally made and apparently well engineered, although this concept never made any real headway against the simpler bogie design of the average six-wheeler.

Preserved Bulldogs

The movement to preserve and restore examples of the millions of motor vehicles which have roamed the nation's highways since the early 1900s has reached epidemic proportions during the 1970s. In addition to the various auto collectors who specialize in early brass era, vintage 1920s, or later classic cars, a growing number are now preserving commercial motor vehicles of all ages, sizes, and body types. The United States Bicentennial Celebration in 1976 gave some further impetus to the restoration of antique trucks by small fleet owners as a way of physically contributing to local festivities.

Bulldogs have become a popular choice among those people preserving and restoring such early trucks, and it is very significant that some of these Macks have been owned by family-run businesses since they were first acquired 30, 40, or even 50 years ago. The New England, Middle Atlantic, and Western States seem to have the highest number of known Bulldogs owned by collectors. However, there are other AC's being preserved in the Midwest and Canada, as well as some European countries such as England and Denmark.

As antique automobile museums and public historical repositories expand their collections, early commercial vehicles have become recognized as a necessary display to show an important step in the development of the motor vehicle, as well as commercial transportation. In 1963 the Smithsonian Institution in Washington, D. C., accepted the gift of a restored 1930 Bulldog Mack dumper, which had participated in the building of the George Washington Bridge and Lincoln Tunnel during the 1930s while in the employ of a New Jersey contractor.

Two AC Macks are displayed at the Circus World Museum in Baraboo, Wisconsin, where one of them still performs a former duty of some circus Bulldogs. Twice a day during the tourist season a Bulldog demonstrates for museum visitors, the technique of loading wagons on railroad flat cars, using twin ramps at the end of a cut of flats. The Fire Museum of Maryland,

Denmark is the home of this World War I Bulldog Mack which has seen many years of service. Note only the wheels and fenders seem to have been modernized.

The 1930 Bulldog being positioned in the Arts & Industries Building, Smithsonian Institution, on August 7, 1963.

at Lutherville, has about a half-dozen Bulldogs in its 50-unit collection of historic fire apparatus. Bulldogs at the Fire Museum range in age from a 1916 high-pressure pumper up to a 1926, 900 gpm pumper, and include a 1917 city service ladder truck. Other Bulldogs are owned by "Kemp's Mack Museum," Hillsboro, New Hampshire; Long Island Automotive Museum, Southampton, New York; and by Mack Trucks, Inc., Allentown, Pennsylvania.

It is thought that the collection of historic Macks at Allentown (now exhibited at the Macungie Plant) will eventually go to a national trucking museum which is being set up under the title of the American Historical Truck Museum. As of early 1979 a permanent site had not been selected. However, it is hoped that with the eventual recognition by the trucking industry and allied interests of the importance of this project, proper backing will be forthcoming. Surely, with the proliferation of antique auto and railroad museums in the country, there is room for one more to present the roots of the American trucking industry and its dynamic contributions to the commonweal.

C|Appendix

MACK MODEL AC SPECIFICATIONS   **FOUR-CYLINDER SERIES 1916 TO 1938**

Chassis Component	3-Speeder 1920	4-Speeder 1927	Narrow Pneumatic 1935
ENGINE:			
Bore and stroke	5x6 inches	5x6 inches	5x6 inches
Piston displacement	471 cu.in.	471 cu. in.	471 cu. in.
Horsepower-SAE formula	40	40	40
Brake horsepower at governed rpm	Over 40	50	74
Governed speed-revolutions per minute	1,000	1,175	1,600
(Allowable hp and rpm raised with engine modifications)			
CLUTCH: Type	Single plate	Single plate	Single plate
TRANSMISSION:			
Speeds forward	3	4	4
Ratio in fourth	—	1.00 to 1	1.00 to 1
Ratio in third	1.00 to 1	1.80 to 1	1.80 to 1
Ratio in second	1.739 to 1	3.35 to 1	3.35 to 1
Ratio in first	3.210 to 1	6.42 to 1	6.42 to 1
Ration in reverse	4.280 to 1	7.66 to 1	7.66 to 1
(Auxiliary and optional transmissions available by 1929)			
AXLES:			
Front-sectional shape	Rectangular	I-Beam	I-Beam
Rear-sectional shape	Rectangular	I-Beam	Tubular
(Thickness of rear section varied with AC model capacity)			
BRAKES:			
Service-location	Jack-shaft	Jack-shaft	Four wheels
Parking-location	Rear wheels	Rear wheels	Transmission
SPRINGS:			
Front-length and width	46"x3½"	48"x3½"	48"x3½"
Rear-length and width	52"x4"	52"x4"	50"x5"
(Number of leaves in springs varied with AC model capacity)			
SOLID TIRE DIAMETERS: (Nominal)			
Standard chassis-front	36"	36"	36"
Standard chassis-rear	40"	40"	40"
Tractor version-front	36"	34"	36"
Tractor version-rear	40"	36"	40"
(Tire diameters varied slightly with make and tire width varied with AC model capacity)			
Standard paint color: (Lead-varnish)	Mack-green	Mack-green	Mack-green

Mack AC (3-Speeder) 1916-1922
Chassis Dimensions by Wheelbases

W—Wheelbase	156"	168"	180"
CA—Cab to rear axle	92"	104"	116"
AF—Axle to end of frame	132"	156"	180"
LP—Load platform	132"	156"	180"
OL—Overall length	225-3/4"	249-3/4"	273-3/4"

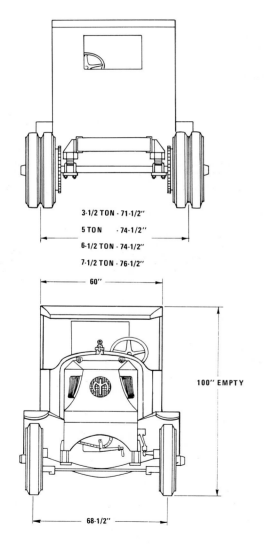

3-1/2 TON - 71-1/2"

5 TON - 74-1/2"

6-1/2 TON - 74-1/2"

7-1/2 TON - 76-1/2"

60"

100" EMPTY

68-1/2"

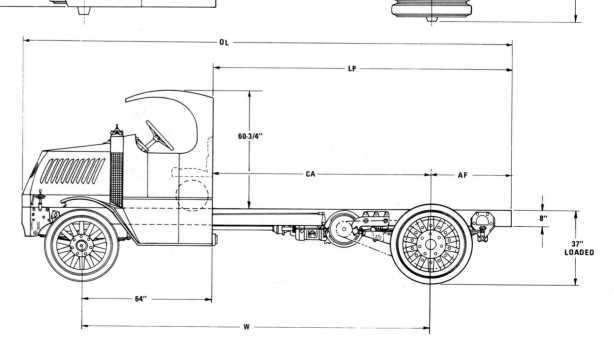

78"

3-1/2 TON - 84-3/8"

5 TON - 89-1/2"

6-1/2 TON - 89-1/2"

7-1/2 TON - 93"

37-1/2"

OL

LP

60-3/4"

CA

AF

8"

37"
LOADED

64"

W

177

Mack AC (4-Speeder) 1922-1934
Chassis Dimensions by Wheelbases

W—Wheelbase	156''	168''	180''
CA—Cab to rear axle	92''	104''	116''
AF—Axle to end of frame	40''	52''	64''
LP—Load platform	132''	156''	180''
OL—Overall length	226''	250''	274''

Other Wheelbases were: 192, 204, 216, 228, and 240 inches, with LP's available in 12 inch increments on each from 168 inches on the 192 inch wheelbase to a maximum of 300 inches on the 240 inch wheelbase.

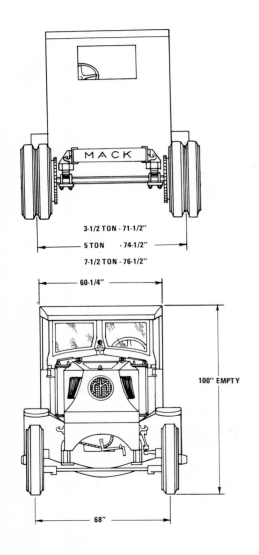

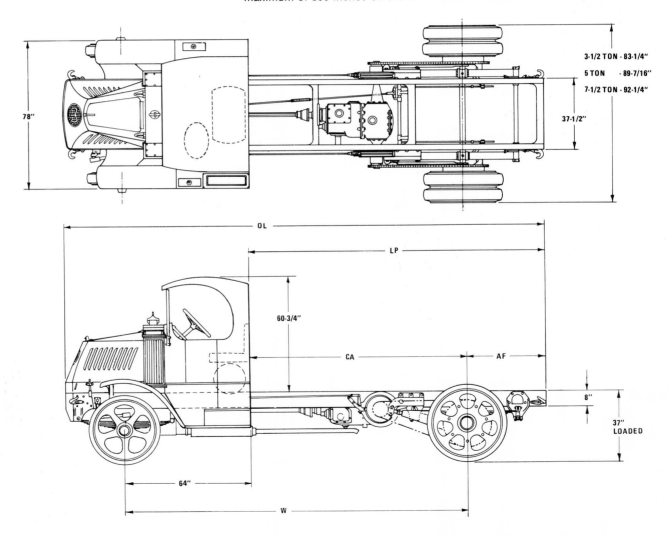

**Mack AC (Narrow Pneumatic) 1934-1938
Chassis Dimensions by Wheelbases**

W—Wheelbase	174"	192"	210"	228"
CA—Cab to rear axle	105"	123"	141"	159"
AF—Axle to end of frame	54"	60"	72"	84"
LP—Load platform	159"	183"	213"	243"
OL—Overall length	257-9/16"	281-9/16"	311-9/16"	341-9/16"

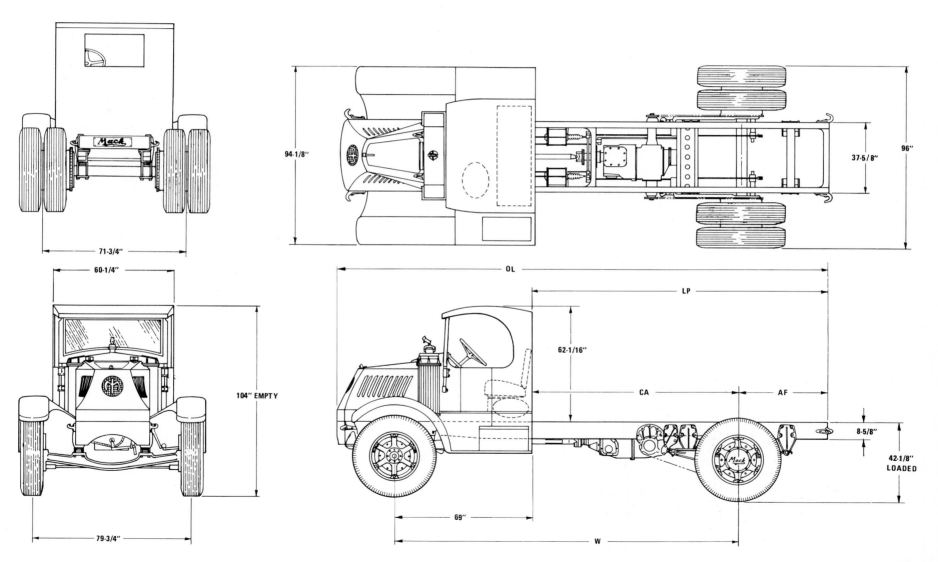

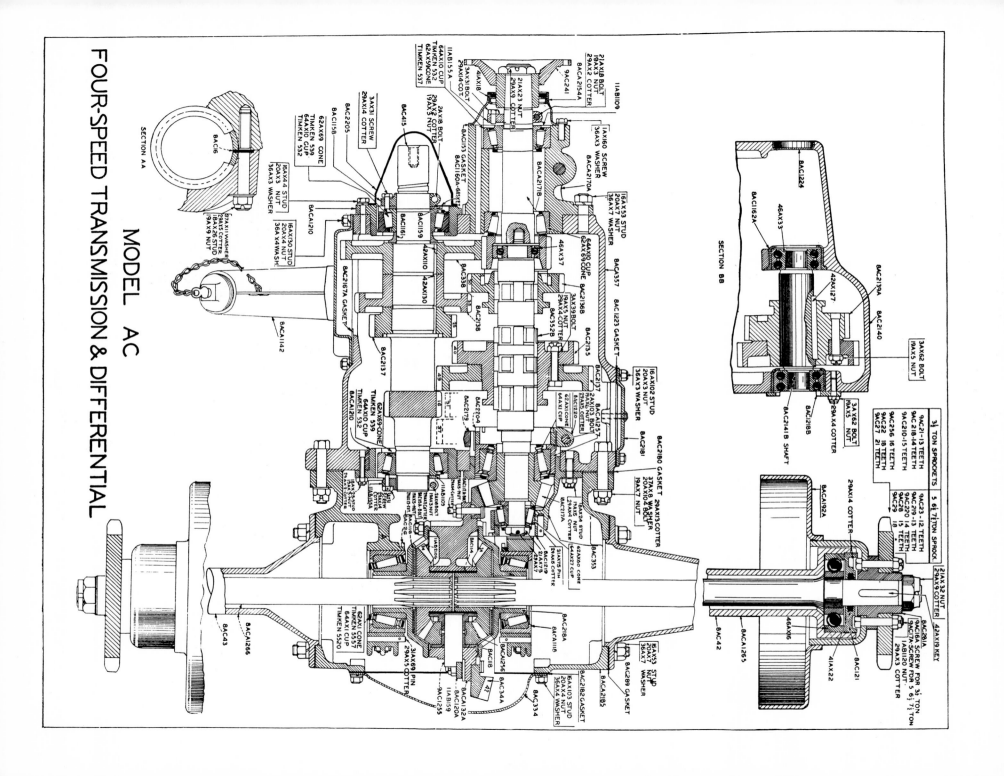

MODEL AC
FOUR-SPEED TRANSMISSION & DIFFERENTIAL

SECTION AA

SECTION BB

The following tables of various Bulldog truck, and related model, chassis numbers have been assembled from several sources. Those numbers for the years prior to 1922 were published in contemporary automotive reference books, and the numbers after 1921 were abstracted from Mack Sales Department chassis ledgers. Chassis numbers for prototype and projected models were obtained from old Pricing Department tables.

Because new vehicles were not sold in the precise order of their chassis number sequences, it is impossible to develop exact annual groupings of such numbers. It is also impossible to develop annual or any other type of production figures from the general chassis number groupings that have been developed, since numbers were cancelled and some vehicles were also built out of their numerical sequence for various reasons.

Therefore, these tables should be used only as a general guide to the approximate period in which a specific chassis may

have been constructed and/or sold. Data on a specific chassis should be requested from: Public Relations Department, Mack Trucks, Inc., Allentown, Penna. 18105.

The location of Bulldog chassis numbers were traditionally on the top flange of the left-hand frame side-rail, at the very front of the chassis. Mack AC chassis numbers were also stamped on a metal plate attached to the right-hand side of the seat-riser in most cabs. Engine numbers were usually located on the left-hand side of the crankcase, and should not be confused with chassis numbers when requesting data on a specific chassis.

Model AC Mack Chassis Numbers
Four-cylinder, Light-duty Series, 1915-1934
Composite Listing of Approximate Dates of Construction

Capacity Rating	Chassis Number Range From	To	Approximate Date of Manufacture From	To	Notes and Explanations
3-½ tons	E-1	E-2	Jan. 1915	June 1915	Prototype test vehicles
3-½ tons	7,000	7,202	Feb. 1916	Dec. 1916	First production units
3-½ tons	7,203	7,376	Jan. 1917	Summer 1917	
3-½ tons	73,000	73,221	Summer 1917	Dec. 1917	Start of new C/N mode
3-½ tons	73,232	73,999	Jan. 1918	Jan. 1919	
3-½ tons	731,000	731,762	Jan. 1919	Dec. 1919	Start of new C/N mode
3-½ tons	731,763	733,054	Jan. 1920	Dec. 1920	
3-½ tons	733,055	733,774	Jan. 1921	Dec. 1921	
3-½ tons	733,775	735,000	Jan. 1922	Dec. 1922	
3-½ tons	735,001	736,000	Jan. 1923	June 1923	
3-½ tons	736,001	737,000	June 1923	Aug. 1924	
3-½ tons	737,001	738,000	Aug. 1924	Jan. 1925	
3-½ tons	738,001	739,000	Jan. 1925	July 1925	
3-½ tons	739,001	739,999	July 1925	Dec. 1925	
3-½ tons	7,310,000	7,311,000	Jan. 1926	June 1926	Start of new C/N mode
3-½ tons	7,311,001	7,312,000	June 1926	July 1928	
3-½ tons	7,312,001	7,313,000	July 1928	Feb. 1929	
3-½ tons	7,313,001	7,313,516	Feb. 1929	Jan. 1930	
Light (5 to 8 tons)	4AC1CL1,001	4AC1CL1,100	Feb. 1930	May 1930	Start of new C/N mode
Light (5 to 8 tons)	4AC1CL1,101	4AC1CL1,200	May 1930	July 1930	
Light (5 to 8 tons)	4AC1CL1,201	4AC1CL1,300	July 1930	Sept. 1931	
Light (5 to 8 tons)	4AC1CL1,301	4AC1CL1,335	Sept. 1931	Apr. 1934	
Fire Apparatus	77,001		(no production recorded)		Dual reduction

Model AC Mack Chassis Numbers
Four-cylinder, Heavy-duty Series, 1916-1934
Composite Listing of Approximate Dates of Construction

Capacity Rating	Chassis Number Range		Approximate Date of Manufacture		Notes and Explanations
7-½ tons	12,000	12,051	Apr. 1916	Dec. 1916	
7-½ tons	12,052	12,152	Jan. 1917	May 1917	
7-½ tons	153,000	153,046	May 1917	Dec. 1917	Start of new C/N mode
7-½ tons	153,047	153,247	Jan. 1918	Dec. 1918	
7-½ tons	153,248	153,751	Jan. 1919	Dec. 1919	
7-½ tons	153,752	153,999	Jan. 1920	June 1920	
7-½ tons	1,531,000	1,531,306	June 1920	Dec. 1920	Start of new C/N mode
7-½ tons	1,531,307	1,531,641	Jan. 1921	Dec. 1921	
7-½ tons	1,531,642	1,531,800	Jan. 1922	Dec. 1922	
7-½ tons	1,531,801	1,532,000	Jan. 1923	Oct. 1923	
7-½ tons	1,532,001	1,532,200	Nov. 1923	July 1924	
7-½ tons	1,532,201	1,532,400	July 1924	Jan. 1925	
7-½ tons	1,532,401	1,532,600	Jan. 1925	Sep. 1925	
7-½ tons	1,532,601	1,532,800	Sep. 1925	Apr. 1926	
7-½ tons	1,532,801	1,533,000	Apr. 1926	Oct. 1926	
7-½ tons	1,533,001	1,533,200	Oct. 1926	May 1927	
7-½ tons	1,533,201	1,533,400	May 1927	Dec. 1927	
7-½ tons	1,533,401	1,533,600	Dec. 1927	Mar. 1929	
7-½ tons	1,533,601	1,533,800	Mar. 1929	May 1929	
7-½ tons	1,533,801	1,533,999	May 1929	Dec. 1929	
Heavy (7 to 10 tons)	4AC1CH1001	4AC1CH1050	Jan. 1930	June 1930	Start of new C/N mode
Heavy (7 to 10 tons)	4AC1CH1051	4AC1CH1100	June 1930	Dec. 1930	
Heavy (7 to 10 tons)	4AC1CH1101	4AC1CH1150	Feb. 1931	Apr. 1932	
Heavy (7 to 10 tons)	4AC1CH1151	4AC1CH1191	Apr. 1932	Oct. 1937	

Model AC Mack Chassis Numbers
Four-cylinder, Miscellaneous Series 1919-1932
Composite Listing of Approximate Dates of Construction

Capacity Rating	Chassis Number Range		Approximate Date of Manufacture		Notes and Explanations
	From	To	From	To	
3-½ to 5 tons	76,007	76,009	Aug. 1928	Aug. 1928	Six-wheel, four-wheel drive
5 tons	106,001	106,018	June 1927	May 1928	Six-wheel, four-wheel drive
5-½ to 7 tons	116,001	116,032	Feb. 1928	June 1930	Six-wheel, four-wheel drive
6-½ tons	136,001		(no production recorded)		Six-wheel, four-wheel drive
7-½ tons	156,001		(no production recorded)		Six-wheel, four-wheel drive
10 tons	206,001	206,115	Mar. 1929	Feb. 1930	Six-wheel, four-wheel drive
10 tons	4AC2C1001	4AC2C1023	Mar. 1930	Sep. 1932	Six-wheel, four-wheel drive
10 tons	4AC7C1001		(only one unit produced)		Six-wheel, two-wheel drive

Capacity Rating	Chassis Number Range		Approximate Date of Manufacture		Notes and Explanations
	From	To	From	To	
5-½ tons worm-drive	114,000	114,043	May 1917	May 1919	Changed to 104,000/043
5 tons worm-drive	104,000	104,029			Remained as worm-drive
5 tons worm-drive	104,030	104,043			Changed to 105,001/014
5 tons dual reduction	105,001	105,014	May 1919	Aug. 1919	Changed from worm-drive

Model AC Mack Chassis Numbers
Six-cylinder, Medium and Heavy-duty Series, 1930-1934
Composite Listing of Approximate Dates of Construction

Model/Rating	Chassis Number Range		Approximate Date of Manufacture		Notes and Explanations
	From	To	From	To	
Medium 6 to 8 tons	6AC1CM1003	6AC1CM1050	Oct. 1930	Feb. 1931	
Medium 6 to 8 tons	6AC1CM1051	6AC1CM1100	Apr. 1931	June 1931	
Medium 6 to 8 tons	6AC1CM1101	6AC1CM1150	June 1931	Nov. 1931	
Medium 6 to 8 tons	6AC1CM1151	6AC1CM1164	Nov. 1931	May 1934	
Heavy 7 to 9 tons	6AC1CH1001	6AC1CH1050	Dec. 1931	June 1931	
Heavy 7 to 9 tons	6AC1CH1051	6AC1CH1100	Mar. 1932	June 1936	
Heavy 7 to 9 tons	6AC1CH1101	6AC1CH1111	June 1936	Feb. 1937	
Light 3-½ to 5 tons	6AC1C1001	6AC1C1013	Nov. 1930	Feb. 1931	
Six-wheeler 8 to 15 tons	6AC2C1001	6AC2C1067	Feb. 1930	Aug. 1936	Six-wheel, four-wheel drive
Six-wheeler 8 to 15 tons	6AC7C1001		June 1932		Six-wheel, two-wheel drive

Model AC Mack Chassis Numbers
Four-cylinder, Medium-duty Series, 1916-1934
Composite Listing of Approximate Dates of Construction

Capacity Rating	Chassis Number Range		Approximate Date of Manufacture		Notes and Explanations
	From	To	From	To	
5 tons	103,001	103,999	Nov. 1919	Sep. 1920	
5 tons	1,031,000	1,032,000	Sep. 1920	Apr. 1922	Start of new C/N mode
5 tons	1,032,001	1,033,000	Apr. 1922	Nov. 1922	
5 tons	1,033,001	1,034,000	Nov. 1922	May 1923	
5 tons	1,034,001	1,035,000	May 1923	Dec. 1923	
5 tons	1,035,001	1,036,000	Dec. 1923	June 1924	
5 tons	1,036,001	1,037,000	June 1924	Jan. 1925	
5 tons	1,037,001	1,038,000	Jan. 1925	Mar. 1925	
5 tons	1,038,001	1,039,000	Apr. 1925	Sep. 1925	
5 tons	1,039,001	1,039,999	Sep. 1925	Oct. 1925	
5 tons	10,310,000	10,311,000	Oct. 1925	Feb. 1926	Start of new C/N mode
5 tons	10,311,001	10,312,000	Feb. 1926	May 1926	
5 tons	10,312,001	10,313,000	May 1926	Oct. 1926	
5 tons	10,313,001	10,314,000	Oct. 1926	Apr. 1927	

Capacity Rating	Chassis Number Range		Approximate Date of Manufacture		Notes and Explanations
	From	To	From	To	
5 tons	10,314,001	10,315,000	Apr. 1927	Jan. 1928	
5 tons	10,315,001	10,315,760	Jan. 1928	June 1928	
Medium (6 to 9 tons)	4AC1CM1001	4AC1CM1300	Jan. 1930	Dec. 1930	Start of new C/N mode
Medium (6 to 9 tons)	4AC1CM1301	4AC1CM1600	Dec. 1930	Feb. 1932	
Medium (6 to 9 tons)	4AC1CM1601	4AC1CM1706	Feb. 1932	Aug. 1934	
5-½ tons	9,000	9,177	Oct. 1916	Dec. 1916	
5-½ tons	9,178	9,550	Jan. 1917	May 1917	
5-½ tons	113,000	113,779	June 1917	Dec. 1917	Start of new C/N mode
5-½ tons	113,780	113,999	Jan. 1918	June 1918	
5-½ tons	1,131,000	1,132,000	June 1918	Sep. 1918	Start of new C/N mode
5-½ tons	1,132,001	1,133,000	Sep. 1918	Dec. 1918	
5-½ tons	1,133,001	1,134,000	Dec. 1918	Mar. 1919	
5-½ tons	1,134,001	1,135,000	Apr. 1919	Mar. 1920	
5-½ tons	1,135,001	1,135,480	Apr. 1920	Dec. 1921	
	(no data available for period 1922 to 1927)				
5-½ tons	11,314,741	11,315,000	Jan. 1928	Apr. 1928	
5-½ tons	11,315,001	11,316,000	Apr. 1928	Oct. 1928	
5-½ tons	11,316,001	11,316,939	Oct. 1928	Jan. 1930	
	Replaced in production by 4AC1CM				
6-½ tons	133,001	133,100	1918	Nov. 1922	
6-½ tons	133,101	133,140	Dec. 1922	Nov. 1924	
6-½ tons	133,141	133,180	Jan. 1925	Feb. 1926	
6-½ tons	133,181	133,226	Feb. 1926	July 1927	
	Replaced in production by 4AC1CM				

Model AC Mack Chassis Numbers
Four and Six Cylinder Units, Last Series, 1934-1938
Composite Listing of Approximate Dates of Construction

Model/Rating	Chassis Number Range		Approximate Date of Manufacture		Notes and Explanations
	From	To	From	To	
AC-4 7 to 9 tons	4AC1CN1001	4AC1CN1050	May 1934	June 1934	
AC-4 7 to 9 tons	4AC1CN1051	4AC1CN1100	Aug. 1934	Mar. 1936	
AC-4 7 to 9 tons	4AC1CN1101	4AC1CN1150	Nov. 1935	Mar. 1937	
AC-4 7 to 9 tons	4AC1CN1151	4AC1CN1189	Apr. 1937	Aug. 1937	
AC-4 7 to 9 tons	4AC1C1001	4AC1C1003	Feb. 1938	Sep. 1938	Last group of four-cyl. AC's
AC-6 7 to 9 tons	6AC1CN1001	6AC1CN1050	July 1934	June 1935	
AC-6 7 to 9 tons	6AC1CN1051	6AC1CN1100	June 1935	Oct. 1937	
AC-6 7 to 9 tons	6AC1CN1101	6AC1CN1118	Oct. 1937	July 1937	
AC-6 7 to 9 tons	6AC1C1001D	6AC1C1011D	Apr. 1938	Apr. 1938	Diesel powered
AC-6 7 to 9 tons	6AC1C1014	6AC1C1020	Dec. 1938	Dec. 1938	Last group of six-cyl. AC's

Model AD, AF, AK, AL and AP Mack Chassis Numbers
Four and Six-cylinder Commercial Units, 1919 to 1938
Composite Listing of Approximate Dates of Construction

Model/Rating	Chassis Number Range		Approximate Date of Manufacture		Notes and Explanations
	From	To	From	To	
AD 3 tons	66,001		1919		Bevel gear prototype
AF 3 tons	68,001		1920		Dual reduction prototype
AK-4 3½ to 5 tons	612,001	612,197	Jan. 1929	Dec. 1929	Chain-drive
AK-4 3½ to 5 tons	4AK1C1001	4AK1C1050	Jan. 1930	Apr. 1930	Start of new C/N mode
AK-4 3½ to 5 tons	4AK1C1051	4AK1C1100	Apr. 1930	June 1930	
AK-4 3½ to 5 tons	4AK1C1101	4AK1C1150	June 1930	Aug. 1930	
AK-4 5 to 8 tons	4AK1C1151	4AK1C1200	Sep. 1930	Sep. 1931	
AK-4 5 to 8 tons	4AK1C1201	4AK1C1220	Sep. 1931	Dec. 1932	
AK-4 3½ to 5 tons	621,001	621,500	Oct. 1927	July 1928	Dual reduction
AK-4 3½ to 5 tons	621,501	622,000	July 1928	Mar. 1929	
AK-4 3½ to 5 tons	622,001	622,500	Mar. 1929	Oct. 1929	
AK-4 3½ to 5 tons	622,501	622,653	Oct. 1929	Dec. 1929	
AK-4 3½ to 5 tons	4AK1S1001	4AK1S1100	Jan. 1930	Mar. 1930	Start of new C/N mode
AK-4 3½ to 5 tons	4AK1S1101	4AK1S1200	Mar. 1930	Apr. 1930	
AK-4 3½ to 5 tons	4AK1S1201	4AK1S1300	Apr. 1930	Aug. 1930	
AK-4 5 to 8 tons	4AK1S1301	4AK1S1400	Aug. 1930	Mar. 1931	
AK-4 5 to 8 tons	4AK1S1401	4AK1S1500	Mar. 1931	Mar. 1933	
AK-4 5 to 8 tons	4AK1S1501	4AK1S1589	Mar. 1933	Apr. 1936	
AK-4 Fire apparatus	611,001		(No production recorded)		Chain-drive
AK-4 Fire apparatus	623,001		(No production recorded)		Dual reduction
AK-6 5 to 8 tons	6AK1C1001	6AK1C1003	Oct. 1930	Aug. 1933	Chain-drive
AK-6 5 to 8 tons	6AK1S1001	6AK1S1100	May 1930	Jan. 1931	Dual reduction
AK-6 6 to 9 tons	6AK1S1101	6AK1S1200	Jan. 1931	May 1931	
AK-6 6 to 9 tons	6AK1S1201	6AK1S1300	May 1931	Oct. 1931	
AK-6 6 to 9 tons	6AK1S1301	6AK1S1400	Oct. 1931	May 1932	
AK-6 6 to 9 tons	6AK1S1401	6AK1S1467	May 1932	June 1936	
AK-6 8 to 15 tons	6AK2S1001	6AK2S1050	Sep. 1932	Aug. 1932	Six-wheel, four-wheel drive
AK-6 8 to 15 tons	6AK2S1051	6AK2S1068	Aug. 1932	June 1936	
AK-6 (not given)	6AK2SL1001		June 1932	(Prototype)	Six-wheel, four-wheel drive
AK-6 8 to 15 tons	6AK7S1001	6AK7S1024	Sep. 1931	July 1932	Six-wheel, two-wheel drive
AL 3½ tons	654,001	654,080	Oct. 1926	Aug. 1928	Capacity approximate
AL (fire apparatus)	655,001	655,015	Aug. 1927	July 1928	Dual reduction

Model/Rating	Chassis Number Range		Approximate Date of Manufacture		Notes and Explanations
	From	To	From	To	
AL (fire apparatus)	656,001	656,002	Apr. 1927	July 1928	Chain-drive
AL 3½ to 5 tons	664,001		no production recorded		Gas-electric drive
AL (fire apparatus)	665,001		no production recorded		Gas-electric drive
AP (fire apparatus)	681,001	681,018	Dec. 1926	Aug. 1928	Chain-drive
AP (fire apparatus)	6AP6C1001	6AP6C1010	Dec. 1930	Mar. 1931	Start of new C/N mode
AP (fire apparatus)	682,001	682,100	May 1927	Dec. 1929	Dual reduction
AP (fire apparatus)	6AP6S1001	6AP6S1072	May 1930	Sep. 1938	Start of new C/N mode
AP 7½ tons	683,001	683,011	Mar. 1929	Dec. 1929	Chain-drive
AP over 7½ tons	6AP1C1001	6AP1C1070	Jan. 1931	June 1938	Start of new C/N mode
AP 6 to 9 tons	6AP1S1001	6AP1S1002	Apr. 1932	Apr. 1932	Dual reduction
AP 7½ to 10 tons	684,001	684,016	Mar. 1929	Jan. 1930	Six wheel, four wheel drive
AP 8 to 15 tons	6AP2C1001	6AP2C1021	May 1930	June 1932	Start of new C/N mode
AP 8 to 15 tons	6AP2S1001	6AP2S1023	Sep. 1931	June 1932	Six wheel, four wheel drive

F|Appendix

Bulldog Toys

The following list of over 200 miniature Bulldog Mack trucks has been compiled with the aid of some knowledgeable collectors. Copies of old manufacturers and jobbers catalogs have also been used, but how many of these toys were actually made is very difficult to determine.

Many of these antique toys are highly prized by collectors, with prices of the scarcer items sky-rocketing in recent years. The value of each toy is dependent upon its rarity, completness, originality of parts, and condition of finish; as the repairing or rèpainting of collector toys tends to decrease their value. Collecting toy trucks has become so popular in recent years, that

replacement parts have now become available for many of the cast iron and die cast models.

Some of the body styles were developed by the toy companies themselves, being variations of actual full-scale designs. However, there were a few cases of body styles that never saw the light of day on full-sized trucks. Most of the toy trucks were painted bright colors, such as red, blue, orange, and green.

The first toy Bulldog trucks were introduced in the early 1920s, and were made from zinc or cast iron. Larger Bulldogs soon followed, being made from heavy-gauge steel, and lithographed tin-plate. Many other materials were used over the years, as the list will indicate. Bulldog models in modern plastics can still be obtained in many local hobby shops, as the interest in miniatures of this unique truck continues to the present day.

Die Cast

Length In Inches	Type, or Body Style	Lettering in bold face type, if any, and/or notations	Maker	Dates Produced	
				From	To
3-1/4	Stake	First version lacks logo and chains	Tootsietoy	1923	1933
3-1/4	Coal	First version lacks logo and chains	Tootsietoy	1923	1933
3-1/4	Tank	First version lacks logo and chains	Tootsietoy	1923	1933

Length In Inches	Type, or Body Style	Lettering (capital letters) with notations	Maker	Dates Produced From	To
2-1/4	Tank		Tootsietoy	1932	1934
3-1/4	Delivery van	U.S. MAIL AIRMAIL SERVICE	Tootsietoy	1931	1933
4-1/4	Delivery van	RAILWAY EXPRESS AGENCY	Tootsietoy	1935	1938
4-1/4	Delivery van	Same as above, but one-piece cab	Tootsietoy	c.1935	1939
3-3/4	Anti-aircraft		Tootsietoy	1931	1941
2-3/4	Searchlight		Tootsietoy	1931	1941
2-1/4	Insurance-Patrol		Tootsietoy	1932	1934
3-7/8	Six-Wheeler	CITY FUEL COMPANY (coal)	Tootsietoy	1934	1935
3-7/8	Six-Wheeler	Same as above, but two-piece cab	Tootsietoy	1936	c.1939
4	Tractor and two semi-trailers	A & P, AMERICAN RAILWAY EXPRESS	Tootsietoy	1929	1932
5-1/2	Tractor and one semi-trailer	LONG DISTANCE HAULING two-piece cab and dual wheels only	Tootsietoy	1933	1935
5-3/8	Tractor and one semi-trailer	EXPRESS (stake semi-trailer)	Tootsietoy	1935	c.1937
5-3/8	Tractor and one semi-trailer	Same as above, but one-piece cab	Tootsietoy	c.1937	1941
11-3/4	Dump Train	Tractor and three carts	Tootsietoy	1933	1941
5-1/2	Tractor and one semi-trailer	DOMACO GASOLINE AND OIL (tanker)	Tootsietoy	1933	1935
5-1/2	Tractor and one semi-trailer	Same as above, but one-piece cab	Tootsietoy	1936	1939
5-1/2	Tractor and one semi-trailer	TOOTSIETOY DAIRY (tanker with dual wheels)	Tootsietoy	1934	1938
13-1/4	Tractor and three trailers	TOOTSIETOY DAIRY (tankers, one semi and two full-trailers)	Tootsietoy	1934	1941
8	Auto-transporter	Carries three autos on slant	Tootsietoy	1941	1941
8-1/2	Auto-transporter	Carries three Buick automobiles	Tootsietoy	1931	1933
10-1/2	Auto-transporter	Carries four Buick automobiles	Tootsietoy	1933	1936
10-1/2	Auto-transporter	Carries three Ford automobiles (has two-piece cab)	Tootsietoy	1934	1935
10-1/2	Auto-transporter	Carries three Ford automobiles	Tootsietoy	1936	1941

(Tootsietoy Bulldogs were copied and adapted by at least one Japanese and two English firms in the 1930s, and since 1976 by Accucast, Inc., of Amherst, New Hampshire.)

Pot Metal

Length In Inches	Type, or Body Style	Lettering (capital letters) with notations	Maker	Dates Produced From	To
3-3/4	Side dumper		Barclay	c.1930	c.1940
4	Rear dumper		Barclay	c.1930	c.1940
2-1/4	Tank	GASOLINE	Barclay	c.1930	c.1940
2-1/4	Tank	GASOLINE—with chains	Barclay	c.1930	c.1940
3-3/4	Transit mixer	CONCRETE MIXER	Barclay	c.1930	c.1940
2-3/8	Troop carrier	U. S. ARMY	Barclay	c.1930	c.1940
2-5/8	Troop carrier	U. S. ARMY—with tow hook	Barclay	c.1930	c.1940
10-1/4	Auto-transporter	With two coupes 2-1/4" long and two tudors 2" long	Barclay	c.1930	c.1940
4	Fire engine	six-wheels with water tower	Savoye	c.1930	c.1935
3-1/4	Covered rack	Body enclosed at rear	N/A	N/A	N/A
3-3/16	Covered rack	Body open at rear	N/A	N/A	N/A
3-3/4	Power shovel	Open cab and fixed body	N/A	N/A	N/A

An introduction to the magical world of Bulldog toys. This 1926 view shows three large Arcade cast iron Bulldogs and one Tootsietoy die cast Mack AC.

Tootsietoy Interchangeable Truck Set was introduced about 1923.

Tootsietoy delivery van from 1935 to 1938 period.

Barclay pot metal side dumper dates from early 1930s.

Length In Inches	Type, or Body Style	Lettering (capital letters) with notations	Maker	Dates Produced From	To
3-1/2	Stake		A.C.W.	c.1928	c.1940
4-3/4	Stake		A.C.W.	c.1928	c.1940
6-3/4	Stake		A.C.W.	c.1928	c.1940
5	Tank	GASOLINE	A.C.W.	c.1928	c.1940
7-1/4	Tank	GASOLINE	A.C.W.	c.1928	c.1940
5-1/2	Dump		Arcade	c.1927	c.1935
6-1/2	Dump		Arcade	1927	1935
7-1/2	Dump		Arcade	1927	1935
8-1/2	Dump		Arcade	1927	1935
12-1/4	Dump	Mack logo on cab—decal	Arcade	1924	1927
12-1/4	Dump	Mack name on cab—cast	Arcade	1926	1942
8-1/2	Hi-lift dump		Arcade	1931	1935
10	Hi-lift dump	COAL stenciled on body	Arcade	1931	1942
9	Side dumper		Arcade	c.1930	1935
6-7/8	Ice	ICE	Arcade	1931	1935
8-1/2	Ice	ICE	Arcade	1931	1935
10-3/4	Ice	ICE	Arcade	1931	1935
8-3/4	Stake		Arcade	1931	1932
11-1/2	Stake	Indicated as milk truck	Arcade	1931	1932
13	Tank		Arcade	c.1925	1930
13	Tank	LUBRITE GASOLINE	Arcade	1925	1930
13	Tank	GASOLINE	Arcade	c.1927	1930
13	Tank (tin)	GASOLINE—stenciled on	Arcade	1930	1942
8 to 12-1/4	Crane	With elevating boom	Arcade	c.1930	1935
12-1/2	Wrecker	WRECKER—stenciled on	Arcade	1930	1935
21	Fire engine		Arcade	1927	1942
9-3/4	Fire engine	Chemical and hose	Arcade	1927	1932
13	Fire engine	Chemical and hose	Arcade	1927	1931
4-1/2	Dump		Champion	c.1929	c.1940
4-3/4	Dump		Champion	c.1929	c.1940
4-3/4	Dump	Sump-type body	Champion	c.1929	c.1940
4-15/16	Dump		Champion	c.1929	c.1940
7	Dump		Champion	c.1929	c.1940
7	Dump	Sump-type body	Champion	c.1929	c.1940
7-3/4	Dump		Champion	c.1929	c.1940
8	Dump		Champion	c.1929	c.1940
6	Express		Champion	c.1929	c.1940
7-1/2	Express		Champion	c.1929	c.1940
4-1/2	Stake		Champion	c.1929	c.1940
4-3/4	Stake		Champion	c.1929	c.1940
5	Stake		Champion	c.1929	c.1940
6-1/2	Stake		Champion	c.1929	c.1940
7-1/2	Stake		Champion	c.1929	c.1940
7-3/4	Stake		Champion	c.1929	c.1940

Length In Inches	Type, or Body Style	Lettering (capital letters) with notations	Maker	Dates Produced From	To
4-3/4	Tank	CHAMPION—GAS	Champion	c.1929	c.1940
8	Tank	CHAMPION GAS & MOTOR OIL	Champion	c.1929	c.1940
8-1/4	Tank		Champion	c.1929	c.1940
4-1/2	Wrecker		Champion	c.1929	c.1940
4-3/4	Wrecker		Champion	c.1929	c.1940
7	Wrecker		Champion	c.1929	c.1940
8-1/2	Wrecker		Champion	c.1929	c.1940
9	Wrecker		Champion	c.1929	c.1940
4-1/4	Dump	Sump-type body	Dent	c.1928	c.1937
5-1/4	Dump	Stationary bed	Dent	c.1928	c.1937
15-1/2	Dump		Dent	c.1928	c.1937
5-1/8	Side dumper		Dent	c.1928	c.1937
7-1/2	Bottom dump	CONTRACTORS—has three mechanically operated buckets	Dent	c.1928	c.1937
10-3/4	Bottom dump	Same design as above	Dent	c.1928	c.1937
6-1/4	Covered rack	2-7/8 inches high	Dent	c.1928	c.1937
6-1/4	Covered rack	3-3/8 inches high	Dent	c.1928	c.1937
10-3/4	Tank	AMERICAN OIL CO.	Dent	c.1928	c.1937
15-1/2	Tank	AMERICAN OIL CO.	Dent	c.1928	c.1937
5-1/4	Fire engine	Motorized steam pumper	Dent	c.1928	c.1937
6-7/8	Fire engine	City service ladder truck with ladders cast into body	Dent	c.1928	c.1937
7	Fire engine	City service ladder truck	Dent	c.1928	c.1937
7-7/8	Fire engine	City service ladder truck with ladders cast into body	Dent	c.1928	c.1937
15	Fire engine	City service ladder truck	Dent	c.1928	c.1937
15	Fire engine	PIONEER—C.S. ladder truck	Dent	c.1928	c.1937
4-1/2	Dump		Hubley	1932	1934
5-1/4	Dump		Hubley	1930	1934
6-1/2	Dump		Hubley	1929	1930
7	Dump		Hubley	1932	1936
7-1/4	Dump		Hubley	1928	1929
8-1/2	Dump		Hubley	1930	1933
8-3/4	Dump		Hubley	1928	1934
11	Dump		Hubley	1928	1941
11	Dump	Key-wound spring motor	Hubley	c.1929	-
3-1/2	Express		Hubley	1930	1931
4-1/4	Express		Hubley	c.1926	1933
4-1/2	Express		Hubley	1932	1933
5-1/2	Express		Hubley	c.1926	1933
6-3/4	Express		Hubley	1932	1933
7	Express		Hubley	1928	1929
8-1/2	Express		Hubley	1928	1929
4-3/4	Covered rack		Hubley	c.1929	-
6-1/4	Covered rack	Driver cast in cab window	Hubley	c.1929	-
3-1/2	Stake		Hubley	1932	c.1934
4-1/2	Stake		Hubley	c.1926	1933
5-1/2	Stake		Hubley	1928	c.1933
4-1/4	Tank		Hubley	1933	1934

Barclay Concrete Mixer also dates from early 1930s.

Pot metal Gasoline tanker from early 1930s is believed to be a Barclay.

These cast iron Bulldogs are counter clockwise from upper left: A.C.W. stake, Hubley utility, Champion wrecker, A.C.W. tank, Hubley dumper, and Hubley stake. All about 4 to 5 inches in length.

Hubley cast iron stake trucks in 3 to 5 inch range.

Length In Inches	Type, or Body Style	Lettering (capital letters) with notations	Maker	Dates Produced From	To
4-1/2	Tank		Hubley	c.1926	1932
5-3/4	Tank		Hubley	1928	1929
6	Tank		Hubley	1933	1934
6-3/4	Tank		Hubley	1928	1929
7	Tank		Hubley	1933	1934
9	Tank		Hubley	1928	1929
11-1/4	Tank		Hubley	1928	1929
3-1/4	Utility	BELL TELEPHONE	Hubley	1932	1934
3-3/4	Utility	BELL TELEPHONE	Hubley	1930	1934
4	Utility	BELL TELEPHONE	Hubley	1932	1936
5-1/2	Utility	BELL TELEPHONE	Hubley	1930	1934
7	Utility	BELL TELEPHONE—with ladder and three digging tools	Hubley	1930	1933
8-1/2	Utility	BELL TELEPHONE—with ladder and three digging tools	Hubley	1930	1936
10	Utility	BELL TELEPHONE—with auger, derrick and windless. Also pulls trailer with ten-inch pole, three digging tools and two ladders	Hubley	1930	1941
8-1/4	Compressor	INGERSOLL-RAND	Hubley	1933	1932
8	Transit mixer	TRUK-MIXER	Hubley	1932	1934
4-1/4	Power shovel		Hubley	1930	1933
7	Power shovel	GENERAL	Hubley	1930	1933
8-1/2	Power shovel	GENERAL	Hubley	1930	1941
10	Power shovel	GENERAL	Hubley	1930	1941
6-3/4	Steam shovel		Hubley	1930	1933
13	Steam shovel	PANAMA	Hubley	1930	1941
11	Military unit	Lays plank road from large spool mounted at rear of chassis	Hubley	1933	1934
11-1/2	Dump		Kenton	c.1926	c.1936
15	Dump		Kenton	c.1926	c.1936
11	Bottom dump	CONTRACTORS	Kenton	c.1926	c.1936
11-1/2	Stake	SPEED	Kenton	c.1926	c.1936
11-1/4	Tank	OIL GAS	Kenton	c.1926	c.1936
6	Moving van		Kenton	c.1926	c.1936
11	Moving van	THE UNITED STATES MOVING VAN— WE MOVE THE NATION	Kenton	c.1926	c.1936
15-1/2	Moving van	Same lettering as above	Kenton	c.1926	c.1936
5-1/2	Tractor and one semi-trailer	N & J on side panel of stake body	North & Judd	1930	1931
5-1/4	Delivery	Steering wheel cast into right cab window	N/A	N/A	N/A
5-1/4	Dump	Steering wheel cast into right cab window	N/A	N/A	N/A
5-1/4	Express	Steering wheel cast into right cab window	N/A	N/A	N/A
5-1/4	Stake	Steering wheel cast into right cab window	N/A	N/A	N/A
7-1/8	Tractor and one semi-trailer	Moving van trailer	N/A	N/A	N/A
7-1/4	Tractor and one semi-trailer	Stake trailer	N/A	N/A	N/A

Pressed Steel

26	Delivery	Screen-sided	American Nat'l	1926	c.1929
26	Express	Open pick-up type	American Nat'l	1926	c.1929

Hubley 10 inch Bell Telephone utility line repair dates from about 1931.

Large cast iron Arcade Gasoline tanker from 1926.

Large Arcade cast iron dumper from 1926.

Pressed steel dumper by Steelcraft, circa 1930.

Length In Inches	Type, or Body Style	Lettering (capital letters) with notations	Maker	Dates Produced From	To
24-1/2	Coal	With side chute	American Nat'l	1926	c.1929
N/A	Dump		American Nat'l	1926	c.1929
26	Rack	With removable rack.	American Nat'l	1926	c.1929
26	Tank		American Nat'l	1926	c.1929
21-1/8	Delivery	SHEFFIELD FARMS CO. SELECT DAIRY PRODUCTS	Corcoran	1929	1932
22-1/2	Dump		Schieble	1930	c.1932
24-1/4	Delivery	Solid sides	Steelcraft	c.1925	c.1932
24-1/4	Delivery	Screen-sided	Steelcraft	c.1925	c.1932
24-1/4	Delivery	Screen-sided with headlights, bumper and dual rear wheels	Steelcraft	c.1925	c.1932
22-1/2	Delivery	U. S. MAIL	Steelcraft	c.1925	1932
25	Dump		Steelcraft	c.1925	c.1932
26-3/4	Dump		Steelcraft	c.1925	c.1932
27-1/2	Dump		Steelcraft	c.1925	c.1932
27-1/2	Dump	With headlights and front bumper	Steelcraft	c.1925	c.1932
24-1/4	Ice	CITY ICE CO.	Steelcraft	c.1925	c.1932
26	Ice	CITY ICE CO.	Steelcraft	c.1925	c.1932
27	Tank		Steelcraft	c.1925	c.1932
23-1/4	Gen. Cargo	ARMY TRUCK	Steelcraft	c.1925	c.1932
25-1/4	Gen. Cargo	ARMY TRUCK	Steelcraft	c.1925	c.1932
26-1/2	Fire engine	CITY FIRE DEPT.—pumper	Steelcraft	c.1925	c.1932
24	Fire engine	CITY FIRE DEPT.—city service ladder truck	Steelcraft	c.1925	c.1932
29	Fire engine	CITY FIRE DEPT.—city service ladder truck	Steelcraft	c.1925	c.1932
24-?	Dump		Toledo	c.1930	—
N/A	Dump		Turner	c.1930	c.1934
N/A	Fire engine	City service ladder truck	Turner	c.1930	c.1934
N/A	Fire engine	Hook and ladder	Turner	c.1930	c.1934

Tin Plate

Length In Inches	Type, or Body Style	Lettering (capital letters) with notations	Maker	Dates Produced From	To
8	Coal	With side chute	Chein	c.1926	c.1940
8-1/4	Pick-up		Chein	c.1926	c.1940
7-1/2	Moving van	HERCULES STORAGE	Chein	c.1926	c.1940
19	Delivery	HERCULES MOTOR EXPRESS LOCAL LONG DISTANCE	Hercules	1928	c.1935
20	Dump		Hercules	1928	c.1935
19-1/2	Ice		Hercules	1928	c.1935
19-1/2	Stake		Hercules	1928	c.1935
19	Tank		Hercules	1928	c.1935
19-1/4	Wrecker	Black and red	Hercules	1928	c.1935
19-1/4	Wrecker	TEXACO—all red with Texaco star	Hercules	1928	c.1935
25-1/4	Crane		Hercules	c.1930	c.1935
18	Transit mixer	READY-MIXED CONCRETE	Hercules	c.1930	c.1935
10-1/4	Stake	MERCHANTS TRANSFER	Marx	c.1928	c.1940
9	Tank	ROYAL OIL CO.	Marx	c.1928	c.1940

Length In Inches	Type, or Body Style	Lettering (capital letters) with notations	Maker	Dates Produced From	To
12-3/4	Tractor and one semi-trailer	BIG LOAD VAN CO.—With little cartons of nationally advertised products.	Marx	c.1928	c.1940
12-1/4	Auto-transporter	Carries three automobiles	Marx	c.1928	c.1940
23	Auto-transporter	Carries three mechanical autos	Marx	c.1928	c.1940
23	Tractor and one semi-trailer	Dump trailer	N/A	N/A	N/A

Cast Aluminum

Length In Inches	Type, or Body Style	Lettering (capital letters) with notations	Maker	Dates Produced From	To
5-1/4	Dump		Dent	c.1928	c.1937
11-3/8	Dump		Pioneers of Progress	1975	—

Pedal Cars

Length In Inches	Type, or Body Style	Lettering (capital letters) with notations	Maker	Dates Produced From	To
63	Dump		American Nat'l	1926	—
N/A	Dump		Steelcraft	1925	c.1935
42	Dump	One-ton model	Steelcraft	1926	c.1935
47-3/4	Dump	Two-ton model	Steelcraft	1926	c.1935
45	Dump		Steelcraft	1926	c.1935
50	Dump	Five-ton model	Steelcraft	1926	c.1935
61	Dump		Steelcraft	1926	c.1935
44-1/2	Dump		N/A—sold by Sears	1937	1941
50-1/2	Fire engine	CITY FIRE DEPT	N/A—sold by Sears	1940	1941

Plastic

Length In Inches	Type, or Body Style	Lettering (capital letters) with notations	Maker	Dates Produced From	To
10-3/4	Dump		Monogram	1976	1977
10-3/4	Log hauler		Monogram	1976	1977
10-3/4	Stake	RINGLING BROS. BARNUM & BAILEY and TIDEWATER TRUCKING CO. decals in kit	Monogram	1973	1977
10-3/4	Tank	TEXACO PETROLEUM PRODUCTS	Monogram	1974	1977
3-3/8	Rack		Jordan	c.1970	c.1975
N/A	Fire engine		Jordan	c.1970	c.1975
7	Express	VEGETABLES	N/A	N/A	N/A
4	Dump	ERIE MINING COMPANY	Con-Cor	1977	—
4	Stake	LONG-BELL	Con-Cor	1977	—
4	Tank	ETHYL CORPORATION	Con-Cor	1977	—
4	Delivery van	RAILWAY EXPRESS AGENCY	Con-Cor	1977	—
4-7/8	Coal	COAL—with side shute	Cragstan	1967	1969
5	Covered rack	FRUITS	Cragstan	1967	1969
4-5/8	Tank	FUEL	Cragstan	1967	1969
5	Moving van	A B C MOVERS	Cragstan	1967	1969

Miscellaneous

Length In Inches	Type, or Body Style	Lettering (capital letters) with notations	Maker	Dates Produced From	To
3-3/4	Express	(Metal and Plastic)	Tootsietoy	c.1950	—
8-3/4	Delivery	TOYTOWN BUILDING CO., THEATRE (Wood and Cardboard)	N/A	N/A	N/A
5-1/4	Dump?	(Pewter on Walnut base)	K. Smykal (distributor)	c.1970	1976

Length In Inches	Type, or Body Style	Lettering (capital letters) with notations	Maker	Dates Produced From	To
5-1/4	Dump?	Same as above	Mack Shop (distributor)	1977	—
6-7/8	Rack	AVON—Glass bottle with one-piece plastic body and load	Avon Products	1974	1976

Steelcraft pedal car Bulldog dumper from 1926.

In the middle '70s Monogram built a series of truck kits based on the Bulldog.

References

References: Chapter I

1 Based on information supplied by John F. Winchester, March 23, 1973.

2 *Motor Coach Age*, Vol. 23, Nos. 7-8, (July-Aug. 1971) p. 8.

3 *Ibid.*

4 Readers wishing detailed information on Mack history prior to 1912, should consult *Mack*, John B. Montville, (Tucson, AZ, AZTEX Corporation, 1979)

5 Information supplied by John F. Winchester, March 28 & June 6, 1973.

6 *New York Times*, April 14, 1929, p. 29.

7 *Commercial Vehicle*, Vol. 9, No. 11, (Jan. 1, 1914) pp. 5 & 6.

8 *Horseless Age*, Vol. 31, No. 11, (March 12, 1913) p. 487.

9 *Ibid.*, Vol. 31, No. 20, (May 14, 1913) p. 885.

10 *Ibid.*, Vol. 32, No. 18, (Oct. 29, 1913) p. 719.

11 *Commercial Vehicle*, Vol. 9, No. 9, (Dec. 1, 1913) p. 11.

12 *Ibid.*, Vol. 10, No. 6, (April 15, 1914) pp. 16 & 22.

13 A detailed account of E. R. Hewitt's family background can be found in his autobiography, *Those Were the Days*, (N. Y., Duell, Sloan & Pearce, 1943)

14 Information supplied by John F. Winchester, March 23, 1973.

15 *Ibid.*, June 5, 1973.

16 *Commercial Vehicle*, Vol. 9, No. 11, (Jan. 1, 1914) pp. 5-10.

17 *Ibid.*, pp. 7 & 8.

18 *Ibid.*, p. 7.

19 Mack Trucks, Inc., *The House of Mack*, (circa 1948) p. 7.

20 *Ibid.*, pp. 7 & 8.

21 Interview with E. R. Hewitt, May 1, 1952.

22 *Motor World*, Vol. 42, No. 3, (Jan. 20, 1915) p. 35.

23 Information supplied by John F. Winchester, June 5, 1973.

24 Mack Trucks, Inc., *History of Mack Trucks*, (circa 1945) p. 33.

25 Mack Trucks, Inc., *The House of Mack*, (circa 1948) p. 8.

26 *S. A. E. Journal*, Vol. 32, No. 6, (June 1933) p. 226.

27 Hewitt, *op. cit.*, p. 221.

28 *Commercial Vehicle*, Vol. 10, No. 12, (July 15, 1914) p. 39.

29 Mack Trucks, Inc., *The Mack Creed*, (circa 1948) p. 8.

30 Information supplied by John F. Winchester, Aug. 17, 1976.

31 *Commercial Vehicle*, Vol. 13, No. 2, (Aug. 15, 1915) p. 25.

32 *Ibid.*, Vol. 14, No. 4, (March 15, 1916) p. 7.

33 *Ibid.*, Vol. 14, No. 1, (Feb. 1, 1916) p. 20.

34 *Ibid.*, Vol. 17, No. 1, (Aug. 1, 1917) pp. 16-19 & 29.

35 *Commercial Car Journal*, Vol. 13, No. 3, (May 15, 1917) p. 21.

36 Walter E. Simmonds, *The Complete Bulldog*, (Chicago, Judy, 1926), pp. 13 & 14.

37 *Commercial Vehicle*, Vol. 17, No. 8, (Nov. 15, 1917) p. 12.

38 William B. Parsons, *The American Engineers in France*, (N. Y., Appleton, 1920) Index.

39 *Automotive Industries*, Vol. 40, No. 1, (Jan. 2, 1919) p. 32.

40 *Fire Engineer*, Vol. 11, No. 2, (Feb. 1919) p. 65.

41 *New York Times*, Dec. 29, 1917, p. 1.

42 *Commercial Vehicle*, Vol. 11, No. 4, (June 1, 1916) p. 34.

43 *Ibid.*, Vol. 18, No. 2, (Feb. 15, 1918) p. 6.

44 *Ibid.*, Vol. 18, No. 12, (July 15, 1918) p. 24.

45 *Ibid.*, Vol. 18, No. 2 (Feb. 15, 1918) p. 6.

46 Mack Trucks, Inc., *History of Mack Trucks*, (circa 1945) p. 39.

47 International Motor Truck Corp., *Annual Report*, 1920.

48 *Commercial Vehicle*, Vol. 16, No. 9, (June 1, 1917) p. 14.

49 International Motor Truck Corp., *Annual Report*, 1920.

50 *New York Times*, May 4, 1919, p. 1.

51 *Ibid.*, Oct. 16, 1919, p. 22.

52 Dwight D. Eisenhower, *At Ease: Stories I Tell to Friends*, (Garden .City, N. Y., Double Day & Co., 1967) pp. 157-166.

References: Chapter II

1 Automobile Manufacturers Association, Inc., *Automobiles of America*, (Detroit, 1961) p. 104.

2 International Motor Co., *The Mack Bulldog*, First Series, Vol. 2, No. 9, (Sept. 1921) p. 5.

3 W. F. Snyder & W. A. Murray, *The Rigs of the Unheralded Heros*, (Balt., Snyder & Murray, 1971) pictures 190, 191, 193, 228 & 286.

4 *The Commercial Vehicle*, Vol. 22, No. 2, (Feb. 15, 1920) pp. 64 & 65.

5 Mack Trucks, Inc., *History of Mack Trucks*, (Circa 1945) p. 39.

6 Automobile Manufacturers Association, *op. cit.*

7 U. S. Patent Office, *Index of Patents 1918*, (Washington, D. C., Gov. Printing Office, 1919)

8 *The Commercial Vehicle*, Vol. 23, No. 12, (Jan. 15, 1921) p. 424.

9 R. L. Kulp, Edit., *History of Mack Rail Motor Cars and Locomotives*, (Allentown, Pa., Lehigh Valley Chap., Natl. Ry. Hist. Soc., 1959) p. 27.

10 *Automobile Topics*, Vol. 65, No. 3, (March 4, 1922) p. 213.

11 International Motor Co., *Mack Rail Cars*, (Sales catalog, circa 1923) p. 13.

12 International Motor Co., *The Mack Bulldog*, First Series, Vol. 2, No. 11, (Nov. 1921) p. 5.

13 *Automotive Industries*, Vol. 42, No. 8, (Feb. 19, 1920) pp. 514-516

14 International Motor Co., *The Mack Bulldog*, First Series, Vol. 2, No. 8, (Aug. 1921) p. 5.

15 *Ibid.*, Vol. 3, No. 2, (March 1922) p. 7.

16 *Ibid.*, Vol. 4, No. 4 (July 1924) p. 2.

17 *Commercial Car Journal*, Vol. 28, No. 4, (Dec. 15, 1924) p. 42.

18 *S. A. E. Journal*, Vol. 14, No. 6, (June 1924) p. 652.

19 Mack Trucks, Inc., *The Mack Bulldog*, First Series, Vol. 4, No.6, (Nov. 1924) p. 4.

20 *The Motor Truck*, Vol. 17, No. 11, (Nov. 1926) p. 17.

21 Interview with Henry Miller, Nov. 19, 1975.

22 Mack Trucks, Inc., *Model AP 150 Horse Power Engine and Drilling Clutch, etc.*, (Sales folder, Dated 2-28)

23 Mack Trucks, Inc., *The Mack Bulldog*, First Series, Vol. 5, No. 8, (Dec. 1926) p.]5.

24 *Motor Transport*, Vol. 29, No. 12, (Jan. 15, 1924) p. 440.

25 Automobile Manufacturers Association, *op. cit.*

26 International Motor Truck Corp. & Mack Trucks, Inc., *Annual Report* for years *1920* and *1926*, respectively.

27 Mack Trucks, Inc., *The Mack Bulldog*, First Series, Vol. 5, No. 5, (June 1926) p. 11.

References: Chapter III

1 Automobile Manufacturers Association, Inc., *Automobiles of America*, (Detroit, 1961) p. 104.

2 *S. A. E. Journal*, Vol. 15, No. 4, (Oct. 1924) p. 278.

3 *Commercial Car Journal*, Vol. 34, No. 6, (Feb. 20, 1928) p. 15.

4 *Ibid*

5 *Ibid.*, Vol. 43, No. 5, (July 1932) pp. 30 & 31.

6 *Automotive Industries*, Vol. 52, No. 11, (Mar. 12, 1925) pp. 496-498.

7 International Motor Co., *Mack Pamphlet No. AK2* (sales booklet dated 12-27) p. 2.

8 Mack Trucks, Inc., *The Mack Bulldog*, First Series, Vol. 6, No. 5, (Dec. 1927) p. 14.

9 *Ibid.*, Vol. 6, No. 7, (Apr. 1928) p. 10.

10 *Commercial Car Journal*, Vol. 35, No. 5, (July 15, 1928) pp. 24 & 25.

11 *Ibid.*, Vol. 38, No. 3, (Nov. 1929) pp. 38 & 39.

12 *Ibid.*, Vol. 36, No. 2, (Oct. 15, 1928) pp. 24 & 25.

13 *Ibid.*, Vol. 39, No. 1, (Mar. 1930) p. 36.

14 R. L. Kulp, Edit., *History of Mack Rail Motor Cars and Locomotives*, (Allentown, Pa., Lehigh Valley Chap., Natl. Ry. Hist. Soc., 1959) p. 35.

15 *Ibid.*, pp. 45 & 47.

16 *Ibid.*, pp. 63 & 65.

17 *Commercial Car Journal*, Vol. 38, No. 1, (Sept. 1929) pp. 34 & 56.

18 J. F. Winchester, *American Society of Civil Engineers -Memoirs*, No. 327, 1933, p. 1.

19 *Ibid.*

20 J. A. Wells, *The Peabody Story*, (Salem, Mass., Essex Institute, 1972) pp. 397-401

21 *Ibid.*, p. 402.

22 *Horseless Age*, Vol. 11, No. 23, (June 10, 1903) p. 674.

23 Winchester, *Op. Cit.*, p. 3.

24 B. H. Vanderveen, *Army Vehicles Directory, to 1940*, (London, Fred. Warne & Co., 1974) p. 297.

25 Mack Trucks, Inc., *Super-Duty*, (Sales folder dated 7-29)

26 *Commercial Car Journal*, Vol. 36, No. 3, (Nov. 15, 1928) p. 11.

27 *Ibid.*, Vol. 38, No. 1, (Sept. 1929) p. 34.

28 E. D. Hendrickson, *History of Truck Suspension-Tandem Suspensions*, (N. Y., S . A. E., 1969) p. 18.

29 Vanderveen, *Op. Cit.*

30 *Commercial Car Journal*, Vol. 35, No. 3, (May 20, 1928) pp. 22 & 23.

31 Automobile Manufacturers Association, Inc., *Op. Cit.*

32 *Ibid.*

[33] *Bus Transportation*, Vol. 7, No. 1, (Jan. 1928) p. 57.

[34] Mack Trucks, Inc., *Annual Report*, 1927.

[35] *Ibid.*, 1929.

[36] Mack Trucks, Inc., *The Mack Bulldog*, First Series, Vol. 7, No. 7, (Mar. 1930) p. 1.

[37] Winchester, *Op. Cit.*, p. 2.

[38] *Ibid.*, p. 5.

[39] *Commercial Car Journal*, Vol. 37, No. 3, (May 1929) p. 56.

[40] A. F. Masury, *Notes on the Graf Zeppelin and Her Transatlantic Attempt*, (N. Y., S. A. E., 1929)

[41] *Bus Transportation*, Vol. 7, No. 6, (June 1928) p. 360.

[42] International Motor Co., *Allentown Mack Bulldog*, Vol. 2, No. 6, (June 1924) p. 2.

References: Chapter IV

[1] *Commercial Car Journal*, Vol. 40, No. 6, (Feb. 1931) pp. 14-16.

[2] Mack Trucks, Inc., *The Mack Bulldog*, First Series, Vol. 7, No. 10, (July 1931) pp. 8 & 9.

[3] *The Story of Rockefeller Center*, (New York, Rockefeller Center, Inc., 1932) p. 23.

[4] Mack Trucks, Inc., *The Mack Bulldog*, First Series, Vol. 7, No. 10, (July 1931) p. 1.

[5] Interview with Henry Miller, Nov. 19, 1975.

[6] Mack Trucks, Inc., *Mack at Hoover Dam*, (Sales folder, dated 3-32)

[7] Aluminum Company of America, undated report on Aluminum dump body development, p. 1.

[8] Mack Trucks, Inc., *Super-Duty Macks Triumph on World's Greatest Construction Projects*, (Sales booklet, dated 11-33) p. 12.

[9] *Ibid.*, p. 6.

[10] *Commercial Car Journal*, Vol. 49, No. 2, (April 1935) p. 10.

[11] Automobile Manufacturers Association, Inc., *Automobiles of America*, (Detroit, 1961) p. 104.

[12] Mack Trucks, Inc., *Mack Model BQ*, (Sales folder, dated 9-32)

[13] Interview with John Sloan, May 6, 1974.

[14] J. Winchester, *American Society of Civil Engineers -Memoirs*, No. 327, 1933, p. 4.

[15] *New York Times*, April 5, 1933, p. 16.

[16] Interview with Henry Miller, Nov. 19, 1975.

[17] *Literary Digest*, Vol. 115, No. 15, (April 15, 1933) p. 3.

[18] *American Legion Magazine*, Vol. 81, No. 2, (Aug. 1966) p. 20.

[19] *Ibid.*, p. 55.

[20] J. Winchester, *Op. Cit.*, p. 7.

[21] U. S. Patent Office, *Index of Patents*, (Washington, D. C., Gov. Printing Office, 1915-1935)

[22] *S. A. E. Journal*, Vol. 32, No. 6, (June 1933) p. 226.

[23] *Ibid.*

[24] *Ibid.*, p. 227.

[25] *Ibid.*, p. 228.

[26] *Ibid.*

[27] J. Winchester, Personal memoir dated April 19, 1933.

[28] *Ibid.*, Vol. 32, No. 5, (May 1933) p. 167.

[29] *Ibid.*, p. 169.

[30] A. M. A., Inc., Automobiles of America, *Op. Cit.*

[31] Mack Trucks, Inc., *Annual Report*, 1934.

[32] *Diesel Power & Transportation*, Vol. 15, No. 9, (Sept. 1937) p. 651.

[33] *Commercial Car Journal*, Vol. 50, No. 6, (Feb. 1936) pp. 32 & 33.

[34] Mack Trucks, Inc., *Annual Report*, 1936.

Index

Fini

Mack Vehicle Registry

Those people owning or knowing of a Mack vehicle (bus, truck, fire apparatus, rail car, etc.) are asked to send the type, model and serial number to the Mack Vehicle Registry. This will help in compiling a list of many of the older Macks, and current, their where-abouts and condition for those wishing to restore and preserve this great marque.

Mack Vehicle Registry, P O Box 50046, Tucson, AZ 85703

AZTEX Corporation—Research Information

This book is part of a continuing research project. Please advise us of any additions or corrections which you come across in reading this volume. Any information, no matter how obscure or seemingly unimportant, is welcomed. In sending information, please make reference to the title and author and mail to:

Editor, AZTEX Corporation, P O Box 50046, Tucson, AZ 85703